The Shakespeare Handbooks

THE SHAKESPEARE HANDBOOKS

Series Editor: John Russell Brown

PUBLISHED

FORTHCOMING

The Shakespeare Handbooks

Richard II

Jeremy Lopez

First published 2009 by
PALGRAVE MACMILLAN

Palgrave Macmillan in the UK is an imprint of Macmillan Publishers Limited,
registered in England, company number 785998, of Houndmills, Basingstoke,
Hampshire RG21 6XS.

Palgrave Macmillan in the US is a division of St Martin's Press LLC,
175 Fifth Avenue, New York, NY 10010.

Palgrave Macmillan is the global academic imprint of the above companies
and has companies and representatives throughout the world.

Palgrave® and Macmillan® are registered trademarks in the United States,
the United Kingdom, Europe and other countries.

ISBN-13: 978–0–230–51749–3 hardback
ISBN-10: 0–230–51749–8 hardback
ISBN-13: 978–0–230–51750–9 paperback
ISBN-10: 0–230–51750–1 paperback

This book is printed on paper suitable for recycling and made from fully
managed and sustained forest sources. Logging, pulping and manufacturing
processes are expected to conform to the environmental regulations of the
country of origin.

A catalogue record for this book is available from the British Library.

A catalog record for this book is available from the Library of Congress.

10 9 8 7 6 5 4 3 2 1
18 17 16 15 14 13 12 11 10 09

Printed and bound in China

Contents

General Editor's Preface

The Shakespeare Handbooks provide an innovative way of studying the plays in performance. The commentaries, which are their core feature, enable a reader to envisage the words of a text unfurling in performance, involving actions and meanings not readily perceived except in rehearsal or performance. The aim is to present the plays in the environment for which they were written and to offer an experience as close as possible to an audience's progressive experience of a production.

While each book has the same range of contents, their authors have been encouraged to shape them according to their own critical and scholarly understanding and their first-hand experience of theatre practice. The various chapters are designed to complement the commentaries: the cultural context of each play is presented together with quotations from original sources; the authority of its text or texts is considered with what is known of the earliest performances; key performances and productions of its subsequent stage history are both described and compared. The aim in all this has been to help readers to develop their own informed and imaginative view of a play in ways that supplement the provision of standard editions and are more user-friendly than detailed stage histories or collections of criticism from diverse sources.

Further volumes are in preparation so that, within a few years, the Shakespeare Handbooks will be available for all the plays that are frequently performed and studied.

John Russell Brown

Preface

In multiple ways, *Richard II* resists interpretive certainty at moments when a reader, or a critic, or a performer most needs and desires it. The play's earliest and most authoritative text (1597) does not contain the extraordinary 150 lines in which Richard himself hands the crown to Bolingbroke. These apparently 'missing' lines have fuelled speculation about the play's possibly controversial involvement in Elizabethan state politics, but only the slenderest threads of evidence tie this speculation to the play itself. Although the play is ostensibly a dramatization of actual events in English history, it is unique among Shakespeare's history plays in representing only a very small portion of the titular monarch's reign, and peculiar for its concern with only the broadest contours of the historical events it does represent. One of only two plays Shakespeare wrote entirely in verse, *Richard II* is, paradoxically, relentless in its anatomization of the dangers and deceptions inherent to poetic speech. To embark upon the project of analyzing and interpreting *Richard II*, then, is to find oneself in a hall of historical, theatrical, and poetic mirrors, where every meaning – tangible and vivid though it may appear – has the potential to turn into its opposite. The work of this *Handbook* is not intended to simplify a reader's journey through this hall of mirrors, but rather to celebrate its dizzying complexity and to provide a partial vocabulary that the reader might use to describe what he or she finds there.

The historical background, historical context, critical reception, and theatrical tradition of *Richard II* are inextricably intertwined, and all together are partially constitutive of the range of meanings available to the modern reader, spectator, or producer of the play. While the 'Commentary' at the centre of this *Handbook* can be read in discrete pieces by a reader interested in the theatrical possibilities of a given passage in the play, it will be most valuable and useful if it is also understood as a point of intersection for the interpretive contexts and forms of meaning discussed in other sections of the book.

Unless otherwise noted, all references to the text of *Richard II* are from the Signet edition, edited by Kenneth Muir (Penguin, 1963).

Acknowledgements

I am grateful to John Russell Brown for giving me the opportunity to write this book, and for his rigorous and generous editorial advice and encouragement. Many thanks are due as well to Sonya Barker and Kitty van Boxel at Palgrave, and Vidhya Jayaprakash at Newgen Imaging Systems for their friendly and efficient assistance at every step of the editorial process.

An Institutional Grant provided by the Social Sciences and Humanities Research Council of Canada allowed me to travel to the Folger Shakespeare Library to work on this book, and a University of Toronto Connaught New Staff Matching Grant provided necessary funds for me to do research in theatre archives in the United Kingdom. I am grateful to Genevieve Love for reading the entire manuscript, to Paul Prescott and Holger Syme for reading parts of it and to all three for helping me to improve it. Katherine Vitale has endured more than her fair share of my ideas about *Richard II*, performance and Shakespeare in general, and has tried valiantly (though perhaps with only limited success) to persuade me to keep the good and discard the bad. My research assistant Julia Bolotina did a huge amount of (often very boring) work without which this book could not have been completed and I am very grateful for her enthusiasm and her thoroughness. All the ideas in this book have, in one way or another, been tested and revised in various classrooms over the past ten years and I am fortunate to have learned a great deal about how to think and talk about a text in terms of performance by working with many excellent students; I would like to record a particular debt of gratitude to my English 220 class at the University of Toronto, 2006–7, for bearing patiently with me and *Richard II* for so many months, and for teaching me so much about the play. Finally, I would like to acknowledge the influence of two great teachers, both of whom have written great essays on *Richard II*: Stephen Booth and the late Scott McMillin.

1 *The Text and Early Performances*

Richard II was probably written and performed sometime between 1595 and 1596; the text was first printed in 1597. The play is the first work in what has come to be known as Shakespeare's second historical 'tetralogy' – the group of four plays spanning the reigns of Richard II, Henry IV, and Henry V. It is likely that Shakespeare began to imagine this tetralogy taking shape as he was writing *Richard II*, but his labours in the mid and late 1590s were not exclusively focused on this historiographic project. *Richard II* and the history plays subsequent to it were contemporaneous with some of Shakespeare's lightest comedies: *A Midsummer Night's Dream, Much Ado about Nothing*, and *As You Like It*. These comedies are about lovers and coupling; they take place in rural or pastoral settings explicitly removed from urban and/or political life; and their plots move toward social harmony. *Richard II*, in its concern with politics, isolation, and social upheaval presents a counterpoint to the comedies of this period, but it is not the only play to do so. During this period Shakespeare also wrote *King John* and *The Merchant of Venice*. While the differences between these two plays and *Richard II* are as important as their similarities, they both share its interest in the isolation (and self-isolation) of a charismatic, self-indulgent, and self-theatricalizing protagonist.

Date and early performances

Shakespeare probably completed *Richard II* sometime later than early 1595, when Samuel Daniel's *The First Fowre Bookes of the Ciuile Warres between the Two Houses of Lancaster and Yorke* was published. Shakespeare seems to have drawn some of his material from this text – in particular his unhistorical conception of the King and

Queen's intimate and tragic relationship. (The historical Richard's Queen was eight years old when she married Richard in 1395.) It is, of course, possible that Shakespeare's play was on the stage *before* October 1594, when Daniel's poem was entered in the Stationers' Register for publication, and thus that Daniel borrowed from Shakespeare rather than the other way around; but scholarly consensus, largely based on the 1597 publication date of Shakespeare's play, continues to be that Shakespeare was the borrower.

Some twentieth-century editors and theatre historians, following the research and conjecture of E. K. Chambers, have argued that a letter from Sir Edward Hoby, inviting Sir Robert Cecil to dinner on 7 December 1595, made reference to a private performance of *Richard II* in honour of the guest. In this letter, Hoby says that 'K. Richard' will 'present him selfe to your vewe'. There is not, unfortunately, sufficient evidence to determine whether Hoby is referring to a play (much less *Shakespeare's* play) rather than a painting, or even a book. Charles R. Forker, however, in his recent Arden edition of the play says that 'the apparently heightened interest in Richard II as a subject in 1595 and earlier' seems to make 'the offer of a recent and probably controversial play' the event to which Hoby was likely referring.

What we can be certain of is that *Richard II* would have been on the stage sometime before 29 August 1597, when it was entered for publication in the Stationers' Register: the title page of this first edition says that the play 'hath beene publikely acted by the right Honourable the Lorde Chamberlaine his Seruants'. If the play premiered prior to April 1597, it would presumably have been acted at the Theatre, a playhouse north of the city walls, built in 1576 by James Burbage, father of the future leading actor of the Chamberlain's Men, Richard Burbage. However, the Theatre closed in April 1597. If *Richard II* was already on the boards, it would have been transferred, with the other Chamberlain's plays to the nearby Curtain (built in 1577), whose stage the Chamberlain's Men rented until the opening of the Globe, south of the city, in 1599. It is also possible that the play premiered shortly before it appeared in print, and that its first performance was at the Curtain. Very little is known about the physical layout of either the Theatre or the Curtain, except that they would have been large, open-air theatres with galleries for seating and a pit for standing around the thrust stage. They also would have been among the oldest and most familiar theatrical landmarks in London at this time, having been in continuous operation for 20 years; indeed the Theatre can be considered the first permanent, purpose-built theatrical structure in London. Thus a trip to Shoreditch to see *Richard II* would have involved the dual and perhaps complementary pleasures of visiting an old familiar place of leisure and recreation, and seeing a nostalgic dramatization of the prehistory of the Tudor dynasty.

The play was printed six times between 1597 and 1623, and may at one point have been the source of controversy on the stage. On 7 February 1601, the night before Queen Elizabeth's former favourite, the Earl of Essex, attempted an ill-fated coup, the Lord Chamberlain's Men were paid by followers of Essex to stage a play about Richard II. The conspirators seem to have thought that the story of a monarch whose poor government impels and perhaps even justifies his deposition would inspire the citizens of London to participate in the uprising. In the event, the conspirators were wrong: there was no public uprising, and Essex was arrested and later beheaded. Augustine Phillips, an actor and shareholder of the Chamberlain's Men, later said, in a deposition given before Essex's trial, that the play was 'so old and long out of use that they should have small or no company at it' but they agreed to play it because of the substantial fee they were paid. Later that year, Elizabeth, talking with her Keeper of the Records, William Lambarde, is reported to have said, 'I am Richard II, know ye not that?' She went on to say, making an apparent but veiled reference to the Essex rebellion, 'this tragedy was played 40tie times in open streets and houses'.

Tempting though it may be to see this conversation as a point of clear intersection between the world of high-stakes politics and the world of the theatre, it is by no means certain that Elizabeth was referring to the theatre in a literal sense, and it is not even certain that the performance commissioned by Essex's supporters was of Shakespeare's play. (The scholarly consensus, however, is that it probably was.) Moreover, there is good reason to believe that the equation between Elizabeth and Richard II to which she referred came not from Shakespeare's (or someone else's) play but from a more recently published prose history of Henry IV by John Hayward. Published in 1599, this work was dedicated to Essex and resulted in the arrest of its author. As with its early texts (see below), the early performance history of *Richard II* is one that allows us to imagine, but never quite confirm, the politically energized and subversive position of the theatre in early modern culture.

During Shakespeare's lifetime, *Richard II* was never, as far as we know, suppressed on the stage, though it may have been censored (see below). Only in 1680, when Charles II ordered the suppression of a production of the play, do we get a definite sense of its potential subversiveness. Even this episode, however, must be treated with circumspection: Charles II suppressed the production because of its apparently deliberate resonance with current events – the return of the exiled Duke of Monmouth, who began to cultivate popular support for his claim as the Protestant heir to the throne; and the recent trial and conviction of William Howard for conspiring to assassinate the King (see Johnson, pp. 505–6). But the production Charles II suppressed was also a typically free adaptation and rewriting by the dramatist Nahum Tate (and one that Tate protested he had constructed with a Royalist bias). The subversiveness of *Shakespeare*'s text might not have been part of this episode at all.

The 1597 Quarto, the 1608 Quarto, and the 1623 Folio

Richard II went through six editions including its first printing and the printing of the First Folio. These editions were printed in 1597, 1598 (two editions), 1608, 1615, and 1623. Three of these editions – 1597, 1608, and 1623 – have independent or semi-independent authority, and the nature of the relationship between them is one of the continually baffling puzzles of Shakespeare scholarship. The solution that one comes up with to solve this textual puzzle partly determines and is partly determined by what one thinks about the play as a piece of politically engaged theatre.

The 1597 Quarto is generally considered the most authoritative text of the play, and it is the text on which almost all modern editions are based, including the Signet edition, which I have used as the basis for my commentary in this Handbook. The most significant difference between the Folio text and the first printed text, Q 1597, is that the Folio contains just over 150 lines (IV.i.154–317 in the Signet) that do not appear in the Quarto. These 150 lines, in which Richard gives his crown to Bolingbroke, amount, in some critical estimations, to the theatrical and thematic heart of the play. But the lines do not appear in Q 1597 or in either of the quartos published in 1598; they do appear in Q 1608, but with some slight differences from how they appear in the Folio. Unlike some other Shakespearean texts that contain what seems like visible evidence of cutting or omission, the deposition scene in Q 1597 makes verbal and theatrical sense without the 150 'missing' lines.

There are at least three different ways of thinking about the relationship between these three texts and the 'missing' 150 lines from IV.i. Perhaps the simplest explanation is that the lines are not actually 'missing' at all in the 1597 text; rather they were not written until sometime between 1598 and 1608. Another possibility is that Shakespeare wrote the lines for the 1595–6 premiere, and that these lines were censored and did not get onto the stage or into print during the last years of Elizabeth's reign, when questions about the childless monarch's successor were both urgent and extremely sensitive. A third possibility is that Shakespeare wrote the lines for the 1595–6 premiere, and that they were performed throughout the play's stage-life but censored in the texts printed during Elizabeth's lifetime.

Of these three possibilities, the second – that the bulk of the deposition scene was censored on both stage and page during Elizabeth's lifetime – has proved most compelling to scholars. Taken in conjunction with the hypothetical connection of *Richard II* to the Essex rebellion, a censorship theory imagines not only Shakespeare but the enterprise of the commercial theatre itself as occupying a central, potentially dangerous place in late Elizabethan political discourse. Such a theory allows us to imagine Richard Burbage – or another of the Chamberlain's Men's major actors – personating Richard II with remarkable effectiveness, electrifying a crowd with his ability to make the historical role resonate with current events, and perhaps setting the authorities on edge with his skill to make the problem of just rule physically vivid to crowds of anxious Londoners. This theory also allows scholars to imagine Shakespeare as a particular kind of genius – one whose works might actually have contained *too much* truth for his present moment, and who thus relied upon audiences of the future (Jacobean audiences for whom succession was not an urgent concern, say, or twenty-first-century scholarly audiences) to set the full range of his intended meanings free.

To imagine that the deposition scene appeared on stage but was censored in print is to imagine a different relationship between the theatre and political discourse. In this scenario, it is print, with its relative permanence and its potential for wide distribution, which can participate dangerously in political debate. The theatre, by contrast, is always highly local and to some extent ephemeral: a performance lasts only as long as itself before it fades into memory; and it is always contained within the walls of the theatre, a space that licenses behaviour that the audience understands cannot exist outside of it. To imagine two versions of *Richard II* during the last years of Elizabeth's reign is to imagine Shakespeare taking advantage of the licensed space of the theatre so as to make political commentary that he perhaps knew would be censored in print. In this version of theatrical and political history, an actor like the one who played Shakespeare's Richard is much freer simply to 'play' his role, and an audience freer simply to enjoy the performance as a re-creation of history. Since the stage king will cease to exist once the play has ended, there is not necessarily the added charge of potential danger as the actor coaxes the audience to sympathize with or to reject the monarch.

Accepting the simplest explanation for the 'missing' deposition scene is not the most appealing option for a Shakespeare scholar. If we imagine that Shakespeare did not write the lines until sometime between the death of Elizabeth and the publication of Q 1608, when they were no longer dangerous, the relationship between Shakespeare, politics, and his art becomes different from the two scenarios outlined so far: we might imagine, for example, a Shakespeare who could have conceived of the deposition scene as it ended up being written, but who avoided writing it at a time when it would have brought him and/or his company into disrepute. Such a Shakespeare is not necessarily an artist whose subversive intellect is bound in by external forces such as the political exigencies of his time; rather, he is a canny and self-interested commercial writer whose interest in political commentary might extend no further than what he can get away with. Such a Shakespeare might have written the 'extra' material in the deposition scene for a revival performance sometime around 1608 with the hope of adding some exciting material to a play that had been considered 'old and long out of use' at least since 1601: this might explain why one version of Q 1608's title page calls attention to the 'new additions of the Parliament Sceane and the deposing of King Richard', and says that the play was *lately* (i.e. recently) acted at the Globe. In this scenario, Shakespeare and the actors in his play are subject to, and/or responsive to, external forces (including commercial concerns), which are either more capable of defining art than we would like to believe, or simply less knowable than we would like to admit. Shakespeare's decision to add 150 lines to his play need not be seen to be political or commercial, or even aesthetic; though the decision certainly might be seen to have had ramifications in all three realms. This decision might have come in response to internal company pressures or personal aesthetic preoccupations that we simply cannot fathom. If we allow ourselves to imagine that the 'missing' lines were simply added after the fact, our idea of 'Shakespeare's theatre', must be understood as a composite picture, some layers of which we cannot see clearly, and some parts of which appear differently depending on when and how we look at them.

A theatrical commentary such as the one at the centre of this book must, I think, take the enigma of *Richard II*'s texts as a given, and use it as a way of energizing an analysis of the multiple interpretive possibilities arising from multiple textual and theatrical scenarios. My commentary is based, as I have noted in the Preface, on the text of the Signet Classics edition, edited by Kenneth Muir in 1963. This is an extremely accessible, well-edited text, which represents the standard editorial line taken on the play from the twentieth into the twenty-first century. Muir's text is based on the 1597 Quarto except in the case of IV.i, where it follows the 1623 Folio. The principle underlying this editorial method of combining pieces from different editions is that Shakespeare's intentions are best represented, textually, by using the best possible versions of the most possible available material. Thus, while it is entirely possible that the play was performed in two (or more) different ways at two (or more) different times, Muir's text strives to embody an 'ideal' version; one that was possibly never performed in this form at all. In effect, Muir's text, like most modern editions, allows for the greatest number of theatrical and interpretive possibilities, while avoiding being attached to a specific theatre-historical moment.

My commentary sometimes attempts to attend to hypothetical theatre-historical specificities: I try to imagine the text as it might have been performed by a sixteenth-century repertory company subject to the dramaturgical and personnel limitations we know to have been a part of the sixteenth-century commercial theatre. Where possible, I also try to attend to textual specificities: analyzing differences in stage directions between the Quartos and the Folio as well as differences in line-readings (the 'missing' lines of IV.i being the most significant instance), I try to imagine two, or even three, different texts as each might have been performed for a sixteenth- or seventeenth-century audience. In general and most frequently, however, I have treated the text(s) of *Richard II* as giving rise to an ideal performance – or multiple ideal performances – which never actually occurred, and might never actually occur. Accepting Muir's conflations of the three texts of *Richard II* where they yield the most complex or interesting reading, arguing with 'original' or editorial stage directions so as to open up interesting alternative possibilities for staging, and alternately (or simultaneously) imagining performances by early modern or modern theatre companies, I hope to help my reader discover *Richard II* as an ever changing experience of an almost limitless, self-renewing potential. At the same time, I want to make it clear that any exploration of this limitless, self-renewing potential in a dramatic text is also always highly limited by the interpreter's own point of view. In the analysis that follows, I am careful to suggest a multiplicity of interpretations, arising from perceiving the play within different combinations of overlapping frameworks. Effectively, I am, much like a director, always arguing for and from a particular perspective on the play. One measure of my success in writing this book might be the degree to which I am able to avoid privileging my own perspective, or even to hide it; one measure of your success in making use of this book might be the degree to which you, as readers, are able to recognize where this perspective peeks through and, if you are so inclined, to disagree with it, or to ignore it.

2 Commentary

Act I

Act I, scene i

1–20 *Richard II* begins with a ponderous clarity. Speaking highly metrically, frequently in rhyme, and in a manner characterized by apposition, repetition, and dilation, Richard draws the first lines of battle in a play that will be preoccupied with division, opposition, and antithesis. In asking John of Gaunt whether he has prepared for the proceedings we are about to see, Richard tells us what these proceedings are: the appeal – an accusation of treason – against Thomas Mowbray, Duke of Norfolk, by Richard's cousin (and Gaunt's son) Henry Bolingbroke, Duke of Hereford, the future King Henry IV. Demonstrating his flair for the theatrical from the outset, Richard prepares us for an exciting confrontation: Bolingbroke and Mowbray will stand 'face to face, / And frowning brow to brow' (I.i.15–16). The image of stark opposition here is complicated by the introduction, two lines later, of an image of equation: 'High stomached are thy *both*, and full of ire, / In rage as deaf as the sea, hasty as fire' (I.i.18–19, emphasis added). As opposite as they are, Bolingbroke and Mowbray are also in some way the same. This kind of paradox is a favourite device of Shakespeare and he will exploit it to maximum effect in *Richard II*, a play that follows the fates of two antagonists, the flamboyant Richard and the understated Bolingbroke, whose distinct identities ultimately come to seem interdependent, and perhaps even interchangeable.

21–9 Bolingbroke and Mowbray speak before we hear their names. Each says the same thing: he wishes Richard long life and happy days. Just as Richard's first lines simultaneously oppose and equate Bolingbroke and Mowbray, Bolingbroke and Mowbray's first

9

lines, spoken before the play tells us who is who, simultaneously insist upon and leave ambiguous their distinct identities. A twenty-first century audience, unfamiliar with whatever sartorial conventions might have distinguished a Duke of Hereford from one of Norfolk, will actually have *more* access than a sixteenth-century audience might have had to the ambiguity that Shakespeare cultivates with this delayed naming. But since the characters are both of noble rank, and since Shakespeare gives them almost identical lines of conventionally hyperbolic praise for Richard, a sixteenth-century audience would probably have been in the position of imperfect understanding as well.

What both a sixteenth and a twenty-first century audience would have to help clarify this potential ambiguity is the person of the actor playing Bolingbroke. The part of Bolingbroke must be cast with one of the strongest actors in the company. Thus, an actor, like the one playing Richard, will probably be immediately recognizable to the audience as an actor who plays major roles. It is likely that the leading actor of the sixteenth century, Richard Burbage, would have played the role of Richard for the Chamberlain's Men in the mid 1590s. We do not know who played Bolingbroke, but it does not seem unlikely that it would have been the actor who would go on to play the antagonist to the great tragic roles played by Burbage: the actor, that is, who might have played Caesar to Burbage's Brutus, Iago to his Othello, Macduff to his Macbeth. Even an audience only vaguely familiar with the historical life of Richard II would have the means to identify the more famous of the two actors walking onto the stage at line 20 as the future usurper of Richard II. Whether or not one of the actors is more obviously Bolingbroke, the important thing about this moment is that Shakespeare requires his audience to guess, or simply to suspend the decision – to allow for the possibility that the more famous actor and the relative unknown, the great usurper and a rebel whose identity has largely been lost to history, might be interchangeable. Moreover, Shakespeare has in this moment set in motion one of his play's most pervasive metatheatrical effects, linking the audience's understanding of historical meaning to its interpretation of theatrical meaning.

30–123 Though Richard names each man in lines 28–9, the dialogue unfolding over the next hundred lines or so does little to distinguish one from the other in any more detailed way. Indeed, in the line *before* he names the two men, Richard introduces a new piece of information that further blurs the boundaries between them: they have come, he says, 'to appeal each other of high treason' (I.i.27). This statement somewhat revises lines 4–6, making the previously useful phrase 'accuser and the accusèd' (I.i.17) suddenly ambiguous. As it turns out, Mowbray does not accuse Bolingbroke of treason; he spends the scene defending himself, and in this way the difference and distancebetween the two men is emphasized. But for each degree to which the gap between the two men is widened, a significant counterforce in the language and the staging insists that we see them at least partially in the same terms. Thus Bolingbroke's 'With a foul traitor's name stuff I thy throat' (I.i.44) is echoed by Mowbray's desire to have 'these terms of treason doubled down [Bolingbroke's] throat' (I.i.57). Mowbray's willingness to meet and fight Bolingbroke even in 'the frozen ridges of the Alps / Or any other ground inhabitable, / Where ever Englishman durst set his foot' (I.i.63–6) is echoed by Bolingbroke's willingness to prove himself in battle, 'Or here or elsewhere to the furthest verge / That ever was surveyed by English eye' (I.i.92–4).

The men's speeches could be performed in such a way as to suggest that they are deliberately echoing one another, throwing words back in one another's face; or they might be performed in such a way as to emphasize the guiding hand of the poet, the deliberately artificial way in which similar verbal conventions of chivalric confrontation are being employed by two different characters. In either case, Bolingbroke's language of attack might come to seem the language of defence, and Mowbray's language of defence the language of attack. Another element that helps build a structure of sameness around the two antagonists is Richard's claim to impartiality: 'He is our subject, Mowbray, so art thou' (I.i.122).

123–64   As they echo one another's language, as they identically praise the king and blame one another, and as they both simultaneously adopt – before the audience and before Richard – the position of accuser as well as accused, Bolingbroke and Mowbray also might move in physical concert. By line 160 each has thrown down his gage – a glove or other token presented as a pledge of combat – and each has taken up the gage of the other. Then at line 162 there is a pause of indeterminate length. Gaunt and Richard order Bolingbroke and Mowbray to throw down the gages they have taken up – to let the challenge go – but Gaunt's impatient question at lines 162–3 indicates that this order is met with obstinate silence and stillness. The tension that builds in this long moment of silence and stillness is perhaps both heightened and broken by a moment of sudden and unexpected physicality if the actor playing Mowbray, responding to Richard's repeated order at line 164, takes line 165 literally and throws himself rather than his gage at Richard's foot. If Mowbray does indeed fall down before Richard, this might be the first moment in the scene where he and Bolingbroke are truly distinguished from one another, where Mowbray's passionate protestation of loyalty and Bolingbroke's confident, unwavering power are conveyed to the audience by means of something other than elaborate rhetorical poses. Of course, physical rhetoric can be a pose as well, and Mowbray's action here might be as hyperbolic and baseless as anything he or Bolingbroke has said previously in the scene. The problem for the audience is that Shakespeare's script denies us almost any information that might be helpful in judging the degree to which Bolingbroke or Mowbray is *not* merely adopting a rhetorical pose.

165 to the end   Though each is adamant in his accusation and/or self-defence, neither gives more than a hazy idea of what exactly he is talking about. Moreover, Richard does very little, in this scene or in the actual combat scene of I.iii, to indicate which claim might have more weight. The stillness of Mowbray and Bolingbroke and their audience – on stage and off – at line 162 might be seen as an emblem or embodiment of the scene's dominant concern or dynamic: stasis. Every movement, gesture, claim, and intention of this scene is brought up against an equal and opposite reaction; every positive is framed in terms of its negative. Even the action Richard and Gaunt demand the appellants take to end their quarrel – throwing down their gages – is identical to the action the appellants performed in order to begin their quarrel. Thus, it is appropriate that Richard's final, apparently decisive action at the end of the scene is really a form of inaction. 'We were not born to sue, but to command', he says at line 196, suggesting a royal contravention of the obstinacy of the two appellants. But his command, that the two men 'Be ready, as your lives shall answer it, / At Coventry upon St. Lambert's day' (I.i.198–9) gives the men what they've been asking for from the start, and what Richard has been attempting to talk them out of: the opportunity for single combat. Of course, we should not be too quick to read this false command as a sign of weakness; such a reading, too, must encounter its opposite. In I.iii Richard will negate the command he makes here and perhaps have the opportunity to demonstrate to his audience (on stage and off) that his acquiescence to Bolingbroke and Mowbray is in fact a calculated strategy with the force of a command – the beginning of a game he will win when he orders the combatants, just moments from striking one another, to stand still.

Act I, scene ii

1–8 John of Gaunt, virtually silent throughout the preceding scene, continues to be rather reticent here. Like his son in the preceding scene, Gaunt is preoccupied with past events whose details are expressed obliquely at best, and more often simply opaquely. His first line, 'Mass, the part I had in Woodstock's blood' (I.ii.1), is meant to be an expression of his sibling relationship with Richard's former nemesis, but might sound like an admission that he played a role in *spilling* Woodstock's blood. (Historically, it is entirely possible that Gaunt knew of and assented to the murder of Woodstock.) Just as Bolingbroke is imprecise in his accusation of the 'lewd employments' for which Mowbray used crown funds (I.i.90) and just as Mowbray is vague in his admission of having lay in ambush for Bolingbroke (I.i.136–8), so Gaunt is highly equivocal when he acknowledges the possibility that the King might be responsible – and thus should be brought to justice – for Woodstock's death.

9–36 The Duchess of Gloucester provides a counterpoint to Gaunt's equivocal vagueness. In her 50 odd lines – her only lines in the entire play – she gives a large amount of specific expository and emotional information that seems reliable *because* it is so specific. From the Duchess we learn that Gaunt and Woodstock were each one of 'Edward's seven sons', one of 'seven fair branches springing from one root' (I.i.11–13); that the 'branch' of Woodstock was 'hacked down ... / By Envy's hand and Murder's bloody ax' (I.ii.20–1); that it is Gaunt's fraternal obligation to avenge his brother, who was 'the model of thy father's life' (I.ii.28); and that the Duchess will not go to Coventry with Gaunt, but rather to an empty and desolate house at Plashy, where grief 'must end her life' (I.ii.55). The Duchess does not actually shed any more light than Gaunt does on the question of who murdered Woodstock; in lines 20–1 she does not specify whose hand wielded the axe. But her numerically precise history of the Lancaster family and her detailed description of the present actions that she will take and that Gaunt *should* take make her understanding of the relationship between past and present more direct and efficient than that of anyone who has spoken so far.

37–41 'God's is the quarrel', Gaunt replies at line 37, suggesting that whatever passed between Richard and his uncle is outside the purview of mortals like himself and the Duchess. He goes on to make it sound as though Richard might have killed Woodstock at God's own request: 'God's substitute, / His deputy appointed in His sight, / Hath caused his death.' In the next half of line 39, however, Gaunt hedges this claim: the phrase 'the which if wrongfully' admits that Richard *might* have fallible mortal agency. Then the next two lines act as a counterweight to the first two, maintaining that if Richard did *not* act as 'God's substitute', only God can punish him for it. The exposition of this scene is, like that of the preceding scene, simultaneously precise and imprecise. Although we get a sense that events in the past – Mowbray's corruption and Woodstock's death – continue to bear urgently upon the present, we do not know *how* exactly these events in the past happened. This is because we only have the slippery rhetoric of a self-interested Bolingbroke, a defensive Mowbray, and a cagey and political John of Gaunt to rely upon.

42 to the end Since this is the Duchess of Gloucester's only appearance in the play, it is the actor's privilege to make a great deal of the role. As local and specific as the character's concerns are, she can be seen to give powerful expression to ideas that preoccupy characters through the rest of the play. Lines 58–61, for example, are the first in a series of passages spread throughout the play where a character attempts to define the nature of grief and sorrow. The particular forcefulness of the Duchess's role would have, in the early modern period, partly derived from the fact that the actor would have been a young boy, probably between the ages of 13 and 18. (Women did not act on the professional English stage in the sixteenth century.) The boy actor's relatively diminutive stature, ornate make-up, and stylized 'feminine' acting would have powerfully contrasted the Duchess's expressions of familial obligation with the circumspect and politically expedient rhetoric of the other characters, played by adult men, introduced so far. I also think that this boy actor might have, according to standard Elizabethan theatrical practice, been asked to play another role later in the play – possibly the role of Richard's Queen (a point I will take up further in the commentary on II.ii and III.iv), but perhaps more likely that of the Duchess of York (a point I will take up further in the commentary on V.ii). Such doubling would have embodied in the person of an actor, and in the machinery of the theatre, the play's concern to show how the Duchess's discussion of Woodstock's death, and what should be done about it, haunts the rest of the action.

In the twenty-first-century theatre, the Duchess of Gloucester is usually played by an adult woman. (One exception was the Globe production, discussed in Chapter 5.). The gender of the actor perhaps allows us to experience more powerfully than Shakespeare's audience could have the counterpoint and contrast between this lone female presence and the otherwise all-male world of the play's first two scenes. An Elizabethan boy actor – who read lines written by male playwrights and learned his craft through apprenticeship to adult male actors – would have always been performing a masculine idea (possibly even a parody) of feminine behaviour. On the contrary, a modern actress might seem unburdened by the need to 'perform' her gender and thus perhaps feel freer to perform the thematic and emotional force of the character's lines in a naturalistic, immediately affecting way. A modern audience might thus experience more powerfully than an early modern audience could have the Duchess's pointedly gendered language as she attempts to make Gaunt feel responsible not only to his dead brother, but to the memory of his mother as well: 'That bed, that womb, / That mettle, that self mould that fashioned thee, / Made him a man' (I.ii.22–4).

Act I, scene iii

1–41   After the tightly focused, intimate, personal scene of I.ii, the play returns to the mode of its first scene: public, political, populous.

Although a quarrel of much greater consequence than that between
Gaunt and the Duchess is being enacted in I.iii, the rhetoric of this
scene is not nearly as passionate or direct. Rather, it is muted by
the elaborate ceremony of the Lists and nearly suffocated within a
dramatic structure characterized by dilation and delay.

The first fifty or so lines of this scene amount to a highly ceremonial recapitulation of the play's first scene. The first scene began with
Richard and Gaunt discussing the imminent arrival of Bolingbroke
and Mowbray; I.iii begins with the Lord Marshal and the Duke of
Aumerle discussing the same thing. The appellants arrive in the
company of the King, who probably takes a place above the stage
from which he will be able to '[throw] his warder down' to stop
the duel at line 117. Once the King is seated – and a production may
choose to make this event take more or less time depending on how
much it wants to insist upon the importance of spectacle and show
to Richard's power – Mowbray and Bolingbroke restate the positions they established in I.i. Once again, the language with which
they express these opposite positions is explicitly similar (see, for
example, the echo between I.iii.23–5 and I.iii.39–41).

42–116   Once the combatants have stated their identities and their
claims, the Lord Marshal announces the rules about touching the lists
(I.iii.42–5). This seems to signal the onset of combat, but the signal
is thwarted when Bolingbroke asks to kiss Richard's hand and take
his leave. This is the first of a number of extended leave-takings in
this scene, and part of a pattern of extended leave-takings throughout the play which begins in the conversation between Gaunt and
the Duchess in I.ii and reaches a climax in Richard's farewell to his
crown in IV.i. Bolingbroke takes his leave of both Richard and his
father and, in doing so, takes the opportunity once again to express
the validity of his claim against Mowbray. In response, Mowbray
takes his leave of Richard and once again proclaims his innocence.
Astonishingly, as the two men take up their positions of combat and
are handed their lances (I.iii.100–4), two Heralds *restate* the men's
identities and their respective appeals (I.iii.104–16). When staged,
the scene was and is probably filled with colour, activity, and the
verisimilar details of medieval combat. (For a twenty-first-century
designer, the scene is a gift, allowing research into and realization
of details such as props, clothing, and scenery for dueling knights,

heralds, the royal entourage in ceremonial regalia, etc.) In narrative terms, however, it is almost static. Over the course of the first hundred lines of the scene, we seem to come no closer to the combat we have been hearing about almost since the play's first line.

117–8 The narrative stasis can have the effect of building suspense. As the ornately costumed combatants lumber into place, bid relatives farewell, proclaim their identities, and have their appeals stated publicly, we are meant to feel the great significance of the slowly approaching but inevitable combat. At last, at line 117, the Marshal gives a definite signal for action: 'Sound trumpets; and set forward the combatants!' The combatants begin to move toward one another, perhaps very slowly, perhaps quite rapidly; lances are raised; the dramatic sounding of music silences and focuses audiences on stage and off; there is perhaps a moment or two where the music has stopped and there is no sound at all but that of the combatants moving toward one another, of weapons being drawn. And then, with sudden but undoubtedly elaborate, self-conscious ceremony, Richard throws down his warder and the long-anticipated combat is stopped before it can begin.

119–43 At the end of I.i Richard established his power to 'command' rather than to 'sue' in a paradoxical way: by ordering Mowbray and Bolingbroke to undertake the combat he had spent the entire scene attempting to talk them out of. In I.iii we discover that Richard might have been fully in control all along, and has by a torturous route subjected the appellants to his will. In I.i, elaborate arguments against combat result in an appointment at the Lists of Coventry; in I.iii, complicated preparations for combat lead only to a royal judgment before the battle can begin. The focus for the next part of the scene is squarely on Richard, and he maintains centre-stage with a self-conscious verbosity that echoes the dilated, frustrating preparation for combat in the preceding 115 lines. The speech in which he tells the combatants what 'with our council we have done' (I.iii.124) is an opportunity for an actor to exploit and manipulate a listening audience's experience of syntactic signals. In this speech, Richard constructs three parallel dependent clauses ('For that...' I.iii.129–32; 'And for ...' I.iii.127–8; 'And for...' I.iii.129–32), the third of which is further extended by means of two subordinate clauses;

all of these clauses, constituting fully fifteen lines, occur before Richard introduces the sentence's main verb ('we banish'). Later in the scene Bolingbroke will marvel at the power of 'one little word' in a king's mouth (I.iii.212); in Richard's self-conscious deferral of 'banish' here we see one way in which his little words take on so much theatrical power.

144–206 Mowbray's response to Richard's order of banishment is a rather loquacious farewell to England (I.iii.154–73), and at lines 174–5 Richard expresses some impatience with having had to listen to someone else speak. He then delays Mowbray's exit with a highly theatrical, as well as theatrically frustrating gesture. Mowbray announces his departure with a couplet ('light/night' I.iii.176–7) that has a feeling of gloomy finality. But as he leaves, perhaps just as he is about to move beyond the boundaries of the stage, Richard stops him and seems to be on the verge of reversing the judgment that he has just made: 'Return again.' There is room here, at the comma after *again* (a comma that is in the 1597 Quarto), for another long pause – like the pause in I.i after Gaunt and Richard command the appellants to throw down their gages, or like the pause after Richard throws down his warder and descends to the level of the appellants; in this pause, I imagine Mowbray turns, slightly hopeful, perhaps, but also deeply suspicious, and walks back to the centre of the stage. Audience and characters wait to see if Richard will again arbitrarily and unexpectedly change the direction of the action. But the direction of the action does not change. Richard is still going to banish Mowbray, but there will be some further delay first. Somewhat unnecessarily and in any case at great syntactic length, Richard orders Bolingbroke and Mowbray to take hold of his sword and swear never to reconcile or 'complot any ill / 'Gainst us, our state, our subjects, or our land' (I.iii.189–90). The physical gesture of grasping the sword again unites the two men even as Richard is insisting upon their lasting division, and it gives them yet another opportunity to restate their appeals (I.iii.197–201). The confrontation between Bolingbroke and Mowbray ends as it began: in stalemate, in stasis, and in a moment of visual opposition that is brought near to equation by the similarity of the men's punishments. Mowbray leaves as he tried to leave the first time, with a final-sounding rhymed couplet.

207–9   For the entire first Act, John of Gaunt is notably tight-lipped where others are loquacious. He is a completely silent presence throughout the first 200 lines of I.iii, participating visibly in the whispered council that results in the appellants' banishment, but otherwise perhaps simply providing the audience a means of judging their own reactions to the proceedings. Referred to as 'time honored' by Richard in the first scene, and establishing himself in the second as both loyal to Richard and circumspect in his loyalty, Gaunt probably seems to be the most legitimately powerful character on the stage – not least because he is given no opportunity in the first act to express, mask, or reiterate self-interest verbosely and rhetorically. We see the how much Gaunt's silent looks can achieve, and how efficiently, when, the moment Mowbray has left the stage, Richard announces that his uncle's 'sad aspect / Hath from the number of [Bolingbroke's] banished years / Plucked four away.'

209–47   Having achieved this small victory silently, Gaunt now becomes the focus of the scene and thus turns out to be as susceptible to the problems of empty, repetitive speech as the rest of the characters in the play. Gaunt now takes Richard's place in drawing out the length of a scene that feels – has felt throughout – at almost every moment like it is going to end. After thanking Richard for mitigating his son's sentence, Gaunt goes on to regret his assent in Bolingbroke's banishment and begins to construe the words he spoke as those of an 'unwilling tongue' (I.iii.244). Richard, suddenly curt and efficient in his speech, dismisses Gaunt and Bolingbroke with a crisp rhyming couplet (I.iii.246–7) and leaves the stage; Aumerle and the Marshal speak couplets of their own, respectively bidding Bolingbroke farewell and offering to accompany him to his point of departure: the dialogue here implies movement, or imminent movement, off the stage since couplets are often used by Shakespeare to end scenes.

248 to the end   But Gaunt delays the movement toward closure, asking the now silent Bolingbroke for more words (I.iii.252–3). The two men spend the remainder of the scene arguing over different ways of labelling the experience of banishment: 'Call it a travel that thou tak'st for pleasure', suggests Gaunt; 'My heart will sigh when

I miscall it so', is the reply (I.iii.261–2). 'Think not the king did banish thee, / But thou the king', Gaunt offers (I.iii.278–9); 'O, who can hold a fire in his hand / By thinking on the frosty Caucasus?' asks Bolingbroke (I.iii.293–4). Stubborn though he may be in his refusal to play his father's word games, Bolingbroke does arrive, in the final lines of the scene, at a way of achieving what Gaunt hopes to achieve – the reconciliation of opposites by replacing one term with its antithesis: 'Whither I wander, boast of this I can / Though banished, yet a true-born Englishman.'

The exit of Gaunt and Bolingbroke has the feeling of a theatrical accomplishment because it comes at the end of a protracted, deliberately frustrating process. The effect of this protracted process is paradoxical in theatrical terms: the repeated false endings, dilated leave-takings, and verbal circumlocutions have made us, the audience, look forward to the end of the scene, the clearing of the stage. In staging the deliberately frustrating persistence of loquacious characters, Shakespeare encourages us to long for what would seem to be antithetical to theatrical experience; in other words, to desire silence and absence.

Act I, scene iv

1–19   The scenes of Act I alternate between public space and private space: in I.i and I.iii, we see Richard in the company of Gaunt, presiding over spectacular political ceremonies calculated to display the power of the monarch over even his mightiest subjects. In I.ii, the actor playing Gaunt has the opportunity to develop a character independently of Richard: when he is alone with the Duchess we see that his political loyalty also involves a wary knowledge of Richard's capacity for violence and its ramifications for his family. In I.iv, we see for the first time Richard alone with the advisers who will be the subject of popular and official complaint later in the play; here we see Richard's self-interest, and his love of performing that self-interest, laid bare.

The first character Richard speaks with in this scene might be as much a performer as Richard is: this is York's son Aumerle, a minor character whose part will gradually increase in importance over the course of the play. Before this scene, Aumerle is directed by the text to appear only in I.iii; though, he certainly might appear as one of the 'Nobles and Attendants' who enter with Richard in I.i. In I.iii, he speaks five lines, the last two of which are an equivocal farewell to Bolingbroke, wherein he may indicate a desire to help the latter in exile (see I.iii.248–9). If this is indeed the way the actor performs Aumerle's final lines in I.iii, he has the opportunity in I.iv to show himself to be playing both sides of the fence, responding to Richard's question about Bolingbroke's departure with a sarcastic pun on '*high* Hereford' (I.iv.3–4). As he goes on to describe the scene of Bolingbroke's departure (I.iv.11–19), Aumerle insists upon his own histrionic skill, telling Richard that, rather than say 'farewell' to Bolingbroke, and so 'profane the word', he decided to pretend to be too overcome with sorrow to speak. It is significant that Aumerle uses the same word to describe his performance that Richard will use (I.iv.28) to describe the performance of Bolingbroke for the common people: *craft*. In this final scene of Act I, we see that even in the case of the most apparently minor characters, in the world of public, political spectacle it is impossible to take even the smallest word, look, or silence at face value.

20–36   As we will see increasingly over the course of the play, Bolingbroke is also a sophisticated and self-conscious actor, and perhaps the first vivid sense we get of that fact comes from Richard in this scene. Giving predictable verbal expression to the attitude we saw manifested physically when he placed himself above the appellants in I.iii. Richard shows himself at lines 20–36 to be contemptuous of and removed from his subjects. He finds it both somewhat amusing and somewhat dangerous that Bolingbroke is able to woo 'poor craftsmen', 'draymen', and 'oyster wenches' – the common people who might well support a rebellion if Bolingbroke were ever allowed to return from exile. At the same time, Richard sees – and is perhaps correct in seeing – Bolingbroke's populism as an act: 'he did *seem* to dive into their hearts' (I.iv.25, emphasis added), and wooed them with the '*craft* of smiles' (I.iv.28, emphasis added). To this point, all we have seen of Bolingbroke has been either framed within the elaborate rhetoric of public chivalric ritual or in reaction to his banishment by Richard. In this scene, Richard gives us a vocabulary of theatricality by which to judge Bolingbroke's actions when he returns to claim what is his.

37–41   The way Green, and later Bushy, responds to Richard's concerns about Bolingbroke can have significant ramifications for the characterization of Richard, both in this scene and for the rest of the play. Bushy and Green serve a chiefly expository function in this scene: Green informs Richard (and the audience) of the Irish rebellion that will shortly take him out of the country; and Bushy brings news of Gaunt's illness. It is typical in productions of *Richard II* for these characters to perform this function with levity and sardonic humour: Green's 'Well, he is gone, and with him go these thoughts' (I.iv.37) is easily spoken as haphazardly dismissive. Like Richard, Green does not understand the magnitude and possible ramifications of Richard's confrontation with Bolingbroke. But while such an interpretation of Green is conventional, it is not the only one available. Green might speak lines 37–41 as though he were motivated by a genuine sense of urgency about the Irish rebellion. Rather than being a flattering sycophant, he might be a competent administrator (historically, this was closer to the truth), concerned that Richard shore up his interests in Ireland; and he might seem visibly dismayed with Richard's plan to fund the Irish campaign by underhanded means. As I will discuss further below, Bushy's lines are also open to at least two different interpretations, and each different interpretation of Richard's councillors can lead to a different interpretation of Richard himself.

42–53   Before we hear from Bushy, however, the actor playing Richard is given the somewhat thankless task of simply expressing directly some of the corruption that plagued the historical King's reign. 'And for our coffers with too great a court / And liberal largess are grown somewhat light, / We are enforced to farm our royal realm / The revenue whereof shall furnish us / For our affairs at hand' Richard says at lines 43–7. Richard, the theatrical King, is here made to express, in a manifestly artificial way, some conventional, broadly accurate, but over-simplified ideas about Richard the historical King. The actor employed as the instrument of this expression must on one hand stand outside the character: acting becomes commentary on the historical and theatrical persons. On the other hand, the actor must also make the artificiality a part of the character: acting becomes an essential element of the personality of this figure, whom an audience understands to be both historically 'real' and a theatrical fiction.

Acting in these two directions at once is a difficult trick to pull off without making the character, or actor, or playwright, or all three, seem excessively self-indulgent. It might be the case that, as he asked the audience to look forward to the end of I.iii, Shakespeare is here asking the audience not to like Richard or the actor playing him. This tricky negotiation between acting as self-indulgence and acting as an essential means of understanding human relationships and historical events is a fundamental problem of the play.

54 to the end   Bushy enters in haste to announce that John of Gaunt is sick. Bushy might speak lines 54–6 excitedly, fully aware that Gaunt's death will mean greater wealth for Richard and his friends. Egged on by his sycophantic friends, Richard might then speak his final lines with self-conscious playfulness: 'Come gentlemen, let's all go visit him', he says, with apparent gravity, 'Pray God we may make haste'. Now there is a pause, and Richard changes the sentence's direction as he makes himself and his followers laugh: '– and come too late!' (I.iv.63–4). If Bushy and Green seem to enjoy and encourage Richard's playfulness, the King might seem unsympathetic to the audience, but he also might seem to be misled – not so much a tyrant as badly counselled and immature.

   This is a standard interpretation of the scene, but an interesting textual variant admits an alternative: while all early Quartos of *Richard II* contain what is, in the Signet edition, the scene's final line, 'Amen!', that line is in none of the Quartos attributed to 'All'. Rather, it is a part of Richard's speech, albeit slightly indented from the left margin. Moreover, the word 'Amen!' does not appear at all in the Folio text. Most modern editions print the word, and attribute it to 'All', but that attribution is a later (mid nineteenth-century) editorial addition. A production that follows the Quarto in making Richard affirm his own desires with an emphatic 'Amen!', or that follows the Folio in omitting the line altogether, might be able emphasize Richard's tyranny by representing the loyalty of Bushy and Green as political rather than personal. Bushy's report about Gaunt might have been spoken with genuine concern: this is a matter Richard must attend to immediately. Bushy and Green might not laugh at Richard's final joke, or they might laugh only politely – perhaps calling attention to the theatrical audience's dangerous willingness to laugh merely because Richard's manipulations of syntax demand it. In this interpretation of the characters, Richard might seem more tyrant than misled King, a self-indulgent performer more interested in amusing his audience than governing his kingdom, whose followers are loyal out of a concern for the stability of the kingdom more than a love of the monarch himself.

Act II

Act II, scene i

1–68   Until II.i, Richard and Gaunt are opposed in speech but united in purpose: Richard is verbose while Gaunt is terse, but both seek to reconcile the appellants in I.i; and Gaunt is part of the council that agrees to banish them in I.iii. In II.i, this state of affairs is reversed: Richard and Gaunt are twins in verbosity even as they become overt political adversaries just before Gaunt's death.

The scene begins with York telling his brother Gaunt not to speak to Richard. Talk is useless, for 'all too late comes counsel to be heard / Where will doth mutiny with wit's regard. / Direct not him whose way himself will choose: / 'Tis breath thou lack'st, and that breath wilt thou lose' (II.i.27–30). Gaunt, however, is intent on using his last breaths to speak as much as possible, and launches into a 40 line 'prophecy' about the fate of 'this England'. This is a speech, whose seemingly endless succession of appositives ('This royal throne … / This earth of majesty … / This other Eden … / This fortress …') makes extraordinary demands upon the breath of the actor, who is also attempting to play the part of an old man 'expiring' almost as he speaks. Gaunt, who is directed to enter 'sick' at the beginning of the scene, might have a place to sit or lie on the stage during this speech, in which case there is a vital tension between his diminished posture and the gathering strength of his words. Alternatively, Gaunt might stand throughout the speech; perhaps, on Shakespeare's stage there was no provision for a chair at this point, in which case there would have been a vital tension between the bodily rhetoric of a dying man and the stubborn willfulness with which he remains standing and speaking. In either case, the act of speaking itself becomes the focus of the scene, and, at least until Richard's entrance, the sheer courage with which Gaunt performs this act might convince a spectator that York is wrong about the power of words.

69–112   Richard enters, perhaps with great ceremonial bustle: a sweep of colour and an entourage of attendants trooping across the stage would insist again upon the antithesis between Gaunt and Richard – one now still and silent, the other in motion and speaking – which Gaunt's verbosity had begun partially to collapse. Richard immediately baits Gaunt: 'What comfort, man? How is't with aged Gaunt?' (II.i.72). Gaunt takes the bait, engaging over the course of his final lines on stage in a series of self-consciously clever verbal contests with Richard. Seemingly with breath to spare, Gaunt revels in making a series of vertiginous rhetorical equations: he connects his physical state with the accidental punning connotations of his name, his sickness with the 'sick' reputation of the king, and he construes Richard's relationship to Edward III and the Black Prince as the 'son's son [who] should destroy his sons'.

113–40   The more verbally ingenious Gaunt becomes in his attacks on Richard, the more he and Richard seem to speak with one voice. We see this most clearly in the rapidly alternating dialogue of lines 89–94, and most surprisingly, and perhaps most importantly, in the strange moment at lines 114–15 where Richard interrupts Gaunt. The moment is strange because even though Richard is interrupting his uncle, he carries on Gaunt's syntax; thus, it is possible to think that in his part of line 115 Richard is referring to *himself* (Gaunt's 'thou') as 'A lunatic, lean-witted fool'. In the passage as it appears in the Signet, which is based upon the 1597 Quarto text, the editor has registered the unsettling continuity between Gaunt's and Richard's syntax by inserting the clarifying stage direction, 'Interrupting'. This stage direction is somewhat redundant: the dash at the end of Gaunt's line indicates fairly clearly that he is being interrupted. The Signet editor seems to be seeking a textual way of signalling, as the structure and sound of the lines might not, that Richard is changing Gaunt's direction rather than following it.

Early editors of the play may have been puzzled by this moment as well. The lines look slightly different in the 1623 Folio text:

> *Gaunt.* Landlord of England art thou and not King:
> Thy state of Law is bondslave to the law,
> And—
> *Richard.* And thou a lunatic lean-witted fool...

The syntax is much clearer here; Richard's interruption comes earlier and introduces a new grammatical construction rather than building upon a previous one. Some modern editions (for example the Norton Complete Works) follow the Folio punctuation. The result is quite possibly an exchange that is easier for actors to speak and audiences to understand. At the same time, if we accept the punctuation of the lines as they appear in the Quarto and the Signet, we might understand Shakespeare to be dramatizing the way in which the contest between Richard and Gaunt has degenerated into one of mutually ineffective, inefficient words, where the polar positions held by the two antagonists are brought closer and closer together by their identically strident and vacuous rhetorical poses. We might see in this dramatization an echo of the anti-climactic conflict between Bolingbroke and Mowbray. Similar to the king he tries in vain to chastise, John of Gaunt – in the eyes of audiences on stage and off – diminishes in power the more he speaks. It is supremely ironic that his final couplet in the play, rhyming *grave* with *have* (II.i.137–8), is immediately echoed, in inverted form, by Richard's *have* and *grave*. In sound as in substance the two men have become mirror images, two lunatic, lean-witted fools.

141–221   In the time between Gaunt's and Richard's exits, the latter's language becomes uncharacteristically, ruthlessly efficient. The same is true of Shakespeare's representation of the sequence of historical events. Only eight lines after he has exited, Gaunt is reported dead. Richard's response to this lasts only two and a half lines (II.i.153–5), and the second half of the third line changes the subject abruptly to the imminent 'Irish wars', which must be funded by the seizure of Gaunt's lands (II.i.155–63). York, who was perhaps a silent part of Richard's entourage in I.i and I.iii, and who spoke for the first time at the beginning of Act II – insisting to Gaunt that speech was useless – now becomes nearly as loquacious, and certainly as ineffectual in his loquacity, as his dead brother.

It is likely that Richard is meant to react with silent but visible fury toward the end of York's first speech, as the older man raises the touchy subject of Richard's inadequacy compared to his father, the Black Prince. It is probably this visibly furious reaction that drives York into theatrically potent silence at line 185. Richard's silence has given him control of the scene, and in the space provided by York's unfinished sentence he is able to project calm, menacing concern, 'Why, uncle, what's the matter?'. York's subsequent 22 lines, beginning with a plea for pardon, relentlessly fold back on themselves, tempering each accusation by phrasing it as a rhetorical question, or by phrasing the consequences of Richard's action as vague hypotheses or veiled threats. Richard seizes upon York's last word, *think*, to demonstrate just how airy and ineffectual his uncle's words are: 'Think what you will, we seize into our hands / His plate, his goods, his money, and his lands' (II.i.209–10). York's response, insisting that he will 'not be by the while' Richard runs his kingdom into the ground, may sound forceful, especially as he exits on a rhymed couplet. But Richard suggests that he knows his uncle's threat to abandon him is mere bluster when, at lines 220–1, he puts York in charge of the country during his absence; and we will see at the end of Act II that York has acquiesced.

222–3   Just before Richard leaves the stage he speaks, for the first time, to the Queen, who has stood silently on stage since she inquired after Gaunt's health at line 71. The Queen is given no lines of reply. Richard's efficiency and haste continues to be the central focus of the scene. The parting of the married couple is not something we see on stage. Modern productions often make the Queen seem entirely hapless in the face of Richard's frivolous excitement: her silence in II.i is used to dramatize her marginal role in the royal marriage. But while the Queen might seem powerless in her marriage at this moment (a view that will be somewhat complicated in II.ii, as I discuss below), she might nevertheless wield a considerable degree of theatrical power. Standing on the margins of the scene, listening to Richard speak but unable to respond, the Queen is something of a surrogate for the audience, and we might look to her as a gauge for our own reactions to Richard, basing our sympathy (or lack of it) toward him in part on the degree to which the Queen seems like his ally, or simply another antagonist.

224 to the end   Bolingbroke and Richard are mirrored opposites throughout the play, constantly made to seem as similar as they are different. Though Bolingbroke is not on stage in this scene, reports of his movements in the final lines show that he has become as unexpectedly efficient as Richard. Condensing six months of history

(February 1399, when Gaunt died, to July 1399, when Bolingbroke returned to England) into a third of a scene, Shakespeare seems unconcerned even with theatrical plausibility, giving the exiled Bolingbroke knowledge of the seizure of his lands apparently just minutes after it has occurred. As a kind of counterweight to this theatrical and historical implausibility we get Northumberland's speech at lines 277–98, the first part of which is a list of names whose purpose is primarily to locate the action of the play in a real and particular historical moment.

Another purpose of Northumberland's list of names is to give a sense of the scope of the rebellion against Richard. Though even a historically literate spectator might have only a vague familiarity with some of the names on this list, the effect of their listing is forceful. It suggests that the world of *Richard II* extends beyond the stage and is populated with figures whose significance does not depend upon our seeing them. The invocation of such figures, and through them of a vivid and bustling offstage political process, helps to insist upon the seriousness of Richard's lapses: the way in which they are a real political problem as well as an interesting theatrical problem. Such a function is served also in this scene by the characters of Ross and Willoughby. These characters appear, at least according to stage directions and speech-headings, for the first time here, and only once more in the play in II.iii. They are minor nobility with no direct effect upon the major events of the play. As with characters such as the Duchess of Gloucester, and Bushy and Green, the very minor status of these roles gives added force to everything they say: what they have to say must be important if Shakespeare is troubling to make them say it before dismissing them from the action of his play. In this way, Ross and Willoughby, who complain of Richard's excessive taxes upon the commons and fines upon the nobles (II.i.246–51), and of his military and civil dissipation (II.i.256–69) become reliable witnesses to those parts of Richard's reign which we never actually see.

Act II, scene ii

1–13   At the beginning of II.ii, Bushy gives us a brief description of the leave-taking (which does not happen on stage) between the King and Queen: 'You promised, when you parted with the King, / To lay aside life-harming heaviness, / And entertain a cheerful disposition'

(II.ii.2–4). While these lines do not preclude the possibility that the Queen is marginalized in her own marriage, they also suggest (as V.i will even more forcefully) that the royal marriage is based upon affection and companionship. Until the moment of their final separation in V.i, the audience never sees the King and Queen act together on stage in such a way as to suggest that their relationship is very important: indeed, the *only* time they are on stage together prior to this scene is in II.i where, as I noted above, they do not even really speak to one another. But, in a way that might be analogous to how he uses the murder of Woodstock, Shakespeare seems to insist upon the importance of this relationship by keeping it off the stage, by denying Richard the opportunity to *perform*, and thus risk rendering unreliable, his affection for his wife.

Simultaneously, Shakespeare allows us to imagine the depth of affection in Richard and the Queen's marriage by presenting a Queen who eschews performance, and who is concerned with what *cannot* be seen. Off stage, the Queen seems to have made a convincing gesture toward ceasing to mourn, but when we see her, she is unable any longer to keep up the pretense: 'To please the King I did: to please myself / I cannot do it' (II.ii.5–6). Rather than attempting to maintain outward forms, the Queen is preoccupied with giving a name and a shape to something as yet invisible: 'Some unborn sorrow ripe in Fortune's womb / Is coming towards me; and my inward soul / With nothing trembles – at something it grieves / More than with parting from my lord the King' (II.ii.10–13). The Queen seems to be presciently aware, as Richard and his friends are not, of the dire consequences of Richard's going to Ireland. She shares this ironic awareness, of course, with the audience, which is why, I think, we are able to accept her importance in the dramatic narrative even if we are aware that she is an entirely unhistorical character. We know that the most important part of this history is what Richard does not yet see coming.

14–27   The way Bushy, Bagot, and Green are represented also has important ramifications for an audience's feelings about Richard, as I have discussed above in my commentary on I.iv. In the first part of this scene, it would seem very difficult to present these three men as frivolous flatterers, even if such a characterization had been adopted in I.iv. Bagot is silent (perhaps respectfully, sympathetically silent in the presence of the Queen's sorrow) until line 128, and Green continues to serve a primarily expository function, conveying information about Bolingbroke's movements in England; he can still seem, as he may have in I.iv, like an efficient administrator concerned not simply for himself but for the fate of the kingdom. Bushy, meanwhile, is given a passage of astonishing complexity and beauty (II.ii.14–20) whose central image gives expression to the method by which Shakespeare uses the Queen to create sympathy with Richard. To look at something directly through your sorrow, Bushy says, is to falsify it: the image is distorted as it is refracted by 'blinding tears'. To see truth, to distinguish form, one most look at things obliquely – what is truly important is that which is not readily seen.

As McMillin (1984) points out, the next part of Bushy's speech actually goes on to undo the metaphor he has just created, and at the end of his speech he is arguing that what is important is what the Queen *sees*: 'More than your lord's departure weep not: more's not seen, / Or if it be, 'tis with false Sorrow's eye, / Which for things true weeps things imaginary' (II.ii.25–7). The conflicted movement of Bushy's speech aligns him closely with the audience. He seems to be trying to work out the same problem as us. He seems to want – and to fall just short of being able – to believe what Shakespeare's introduction of the Queen makes us want to believe: that with respect to Richard's managing of his kingdom, there is more than meets the eye; what we see of Richard's performance is balanced by the behaviour to which the stage does not or cannot provide us access. Bushy may indeed be right: V.i will show us that Richard and the Queen *do* (or did) have a good marriage. But at that point, it doesn't matter.

27–72   As I noted in my commentary on I.ii, it is possible that the Lord Chamberlain's Men doubled the roles of the Queen and the Duchess of Gloucester in their sixteenth-century productions of this play. Whether or not they did, it is entirely possible for a modern theatre company to employ this double, and doing so might be seen to have considerable thematic and structural merit. Both women are given vivid metaphorical expression to the *heaviness* of grief. For the Duchess, 'grief boundeth where it falls, / Not with empty hollowness, but with weight' (I.ii.58–9); for the Queen, sorrow is like an unborn child 'derived from some forefather grief' (II.ii.35) and ultimately delivered – in the form of the news of Bolingbroke's return – by the 'midwife' Green (II.ii.62–6). It is significant that Richard's Queen, who was childless, uses the image of wombs and pregnancy to define her central, inward sorrow. There is an echo in this imagery of the Duchess of Gloucester's concern with Lancastrian genealogy and the shared womb of Woodstock and Gaunt (see I.ii.9–36). A crucial difference between the two women is that the Duchess of Gloucester's sorrow derives from Richard's past, while the Queen's is a product of his future. To double these two characters might be to suggest, by means of the embodiment made possible by theatrical convention, that the continuity between past and present – and the effect of both upon the present – can most clearly (if futilely) be expressed by the marginalized female voice.

73–121 Whatever else this scene does to characterize Richard's reign, it also dramatizes, in contrast to what we see of the rebels at the end of II.i, the military unpreparedness of Richard's faction. In II.i Northumberland, Willoughby, and Ross comment upon the king's unwarlike nature (II.i.252–5), and Northumberland demonstrates an awareness of the movements of Bolingbroke, the troops of his supporters, and the Ireland-bound Richard. In II.ii, by contrast, York appears with 'signs of war about his aged neck' (II ii.74) but immediately expresses his belief that he is unfit to rule in Richard's absence (II.ii.82–5). We learn from a servant that York had sent to his son for aid in the battle, and that the servant was unable to find Aumerle; York is then informed belatedly of the Duchess of Gloucester's death (II ii.93–7), just as he is about to send to her for money to help fight Bolingbroke. Perhaps York's most potent line in the scene is the stark 'I know not what to do' at line 100. His provision for the gathering of military forces (II.ii.117) is notably more vague than Northumberland's list of names in II.i; and his last lines in the scene express conflicted purpose and a sense of hopelessness. This part of the scene, with its bustling entrances and chaotic exposition, provides a marked contrast to the luxurious poetry of the first part. It suggests that the sorrow of Richard, his Queen, and his followers, will take on new and dangerous shapes, whether or not those shapes can be defined in metaphors.

122 to the end If Bushy and Green have up to this point seemed like competent administrators, trying to maintain order against a tide of civil unrest, the final lines of the scene allow the possibility that they might seem to show their true colours and to become the self-interested caterpillars that Bolingbroke and others describe them to be. In spite of York's order at line 117, Bushy and Green do *not* go to muster men, but rather decide to take 'refuge' (II.ii.134) from the coming rebels and the 'hateful commons' (II.ii.138). This decision need not be interpreted unsympathetically, of course; York's part of the scene might have made it abundantly clear that Richard's side has no chance, and his friends here might be represented as reluctantly resorting to self-protection at the point when they have no other alternative.

At the same time, the action of Bagot, whose lines in this scene are his first in the play, might at least potentially serve to cast Bushy and Green in a new light. Although Bagot shows the same concern that Bushy and Green do about the potentially dangerous consequences of their affiliation with the King, he decides not to accompany them to Bristow Castle, but rather to go 'to Ireland to his Majesty' (II.ii.140). Perhaps Bushy and Green react to this announcement with a slight start, and perhaps Bushy's 'Well, we may meet again' at line 148 is an attempt to suggest, with false confidence, that the situation might not be as dire as Bagot is painting it, and that he and Green are justified in their actions because they plan only to ride out a temporary storm. Bagot is resolutely pessimistic in the scene's final line. The enduring loyalty to Richard suggested by this pessimism might be part of the way in which the audience is made to see in retrospect (perhaps obliquely, or by indirection) that Bushy and Green have simply been biding their time, trying to see which way the wind is blowing.

The interpretation I have just sketched out for the presentation of Bagot, and his difference from Bushy and Green, is plausible up until the end of II.iii. My commentary on III.i and IV.i will go some way toward showing how developments in the narrative unexpectedly turn this interpretation on its head.

Act II, scene iii

1–35   In II.iii, the actor playing Bolingbroke has the opportunity to re-establish his theatrical presence as a tight-lipped, circumspect politician. In one respect, Bolingbroke is temporarily of place in

England and is dependent upon Northumberland for geographical and political information. We might see this dependence dramatized in his repeated expository questions: 'How far is it my lord, to Berkeley now?' (II.iii.1); 'But who comes here?' (II.iii.20); 'But who comes here?' (II.iii.67). At the same time, Bolingbroke's watchful attitude always allows him to maintain a high level of authority and control. In lines 3–18, Northumberland is humble about his ability to navigate the Gloucestershire countryside, and seems to tie himself in polite syntactic knots as he tries to tell Bolingbroke how much he enjoys his company. The length of Northumberland's speech is set in stark relief by the two lines (II.iii.19–20), with which Bolingbroke expresses his own pleasure with Northumberland's company. Bolingbroke then stands by silently – occupying a perspective similar to that of the audience – during the conversation between Hotspur and Northumberland in which the revolt of Worcester is described (II.iii.22–35).

36–56 A dynamic contrast to the restrained, polite communication between Bolingbroke and Northumberland is probably provided by the new character introduced in this scene, young Harry Percy, or Hotspur. It is impossible to say whether when Shakespeare wrote *Richard II* he had in mind the irrepressible, impatient, forthright character that he would go on to create for Hotspur in *1 Henry IV*; the 20 lines Percy speaks in this scene amount to about half of the lines he speaks in the entire play, and these lines cannot be said to contain any overt hints of the vividly particularized voice Shakespeare gives the character in the later play. An early modern actor would have had historical accounts of Percy's hot-headed volubility to guide his construction of the character; a modern actor has the benefit of *1 Henry IV* and its performance tradition. In modern productions, the Harry Percy of *Richard II* is almost invariably presented as a precursor to the Harry Percy of *1 Henry IV*. He is frequently given a broad Northern accent, and represented to be so excited about the impending military conflict that he does not even notice that Bolingbroke is on stage. His response to his father's question about whether he has forgot the Duke of Hereford (II.iii.37–8) is generally played for a laugh: this is the unadulterated chivalric warrior, simple but noble in his willingness to show 'approved service and desert' (II.iii.44) to the leader of a just cause. In 1 *Henry IV* Bolingbroke, now King, will of course betray Hotspur's noble simplicity.

If the Hotspur-actor plays the character as irrepressible, and makes the audience feel the excitement of combat in a just cause, then he might serve the function of setting that audience up for disappointment – for a shattering of its rather naïve ideals – as Henry IV's ruthless political machinations grind under his most earnest supporters. Alternatively, the Hotspur actor might follow the signals of the text of *Richard II* and play the role in an understated fashion: he might be sincerely humble in his claim that his service is 'tender, raw, and young' (II.iii.42), and might see the process of helping an uncertain rebellion to succeed as a process of growing into a certainty about his own abilities. This might, in turn, affect the characterization of Hotspur in 1 *Henry IV*: there, he would be not simply a 'pure' warrior, whose inherent idealism ultimately destroys him, but rather a particularly loyal subject, who cut his teeth in the service of the new King, and whose fiery opposition to that King is motivated by the extraordinarily cynical way in which his own loyalty was overlooked and turned against him.

57–80 Ross and Willoughby enter, 'fiery red with haste', and for a moment Bolingbroke's language becomes opaque, as though he is not absolutely certain of their loyalty. The word *love* in 'I wot your love pursues / A banished traitor' (II.iii.59–60) could refer to their love for him, or their love for Richard. Lines 61–3 then express in a somewhat convoluted fashion the promise of a monetary reward for those who assist Bolingbroke in reclaiming what is his. Ross and Willoughby reply with a version of the elaborate politeness that characterized Northumberland's speech, suggesting that material reward is the furthest thing from their minds: 'Your presence makes us rich, most noble lord' (II.iii.63). Conversation upon Bolingbroke's return to England is marked by an almost dangerously optimistic politeness, as all those who have been so frustrated with Richard's reign stake their future hopes upon the promise of Bolingbroke's success and his generosity.

One character in this scene is not optimistic or polite, and that is Berkeley, who enters at line 68, with a message for Bolingbroke, to whom he pointedly refers by his stripped-down title, 'Hereford'. Overtly challenged for the first time in the scene, Bolingbroke responds equally pointedly (II.iii.70–3), refusing to talk with Berkeley until he is properly addressed as Lancaster. Berkeley is unintimidated – so much that he is willing to taunt Bolingbroke, punning the word *title* with the trivializing word *tittle* at line 75, and sarcastically offering to refer to Bolingbroke as any lord he pleases at line 76. This is Berkeley's only appearance in the play, and the eight lines he speaks are a gift to a good actor: they express a hard-edged moral sensibility, a concern with 'native peace' over personal gain, that is entirely lacking in the other characters who rush to help Bolingbroke in this scene. Berkeley can give the audience a sense of alternative possibilities to expedient violence and rebellion, and his willingness to confront Bolingbroke directly suggests that the latter might be forced to show his hand here. Unfortunately for Berkeley and the native peace of England, the confrontation is interrupted before it can really get underway: York enters and Bolingbroke can coolly dismiss Berkeley (II iii.81–2), making his righteous anger seem rash and misdirected.

81 to the end   When York enters, the language and energy of the scene shift from the steely implication of diplomacy to the passionate, but utterly ineffectual, rhetoric of familial obligation. The impossibility of York's position is dramatized and expressed by his awareness of the impossible position of everyone else. No other character in the play is as concerned as York about finding solutions to the problems of others, and no other character is so powerless.

The conversation between York, Bolingbroke, and Northumberland is a veritable fugue: York sounds the main theme of just action and restraint. He speaks the reasonable truths that the audience wants to believe: that rebellion is wrong and that what Richard has done to Bolingbroke can be rectified by more noble and peaceful means. Bolingbroke provides the counterpoint, rearranging and recasting York's words – 'As I was banished, I was banished Hereford / But as I come, I come for Lancaster' (II.iii.112–13) – in such a way as to make the dissonances seem harmonious. In the end, York has no choice but to sing his nephew's tune. Northumberland, meanwhile, provides a quietly pulsing third voice: each of his two speeches begins 'The noble Duke' (II.iii.136, 147), and the second one expresses the self-protective impulse that will gradually bring him into conflict with Bolingbroke: 'The noble Duke hath sworn his coming is / But for his own; and for the right of that / We all have strongly sworn to give him aid: / And let him never see joy that breaks that oath' (II. iii.147–50). In this speech, 'that oath' technically refers to the oath that Northumberland made to help Bolingbroke, but it can also be seen to refer to Bolingbroke's oath that he came only 'for his own'. By the end of the play, the curse Northumberland would wish upon disloyal followers ('let him never see joy') is one he likely wishes upon Bolingbroke.

York's final two couplets see-saw between resigned acquiescence and half-hearted resistance, and in this way the final lines of the scene epitomize the movement of the play: from vivid opposition to disappointing truce, from passionate rhetoric to hollow equivocation.

Act II, scene iv

1 to the end   Like so many scenes in this play, II.iv is structured around and concerned with false starts, leave-takings, and delay. The scene's two characters have hardly settled themselves upon the stage before one of them, the Captain, announces his intention to depart (II.iv.4). The reason for the Captain's imminent departure is the delayed *arrival* of King Richard. Salisbury is able, briefly, to delay the departure of the Captain (II.iv.5–6), but the final lines of the Captain's subsequent speech reveal that he was, perhaps, merely being expediently polite at the beginning of the scene: his countrymen have *already* 'gone and fled, / As well assured Richard their king is dead' (II.iv.16–17). The Signet edition directs the Captain to exit at this point, but no such direction exists in any early text. While this is a perfectly plausible moment for the Captain to exit, it also might be in keeping with the play's representation of frustrated action for him to remain on stage, half in the scene and half out of it, while Salisbury speaks the scene's final speech.

Bracketed stage directions at the head of this scene in modern editions often indicate that it takes place 'In Wales', where Richard was expected to land after his return from Ireland. Yet, an audience, especially one in a sixteenth-century theatre, would not have the benefit of such a clear marker of location. What Shakespeare and his company probably relied upon to help indicate the change of location was the accent of the Welsh Captain; the scene takes the audience to a new aural, if not necessarily a new visual, landscape.

This is true in another way as well. The language of the scene looks ahead to the language of supernatural upheaval in *Macbeth*, and is particularly striking following upon the naturalistic political language of the previous scene. These minor characters – neither appears again in the play – are reliable according to the same theatrical principles hat make Ross and Willoughby reliable (see commentary on II.i above), but in something like another dimension. Salisbury and the Welsh Captain, whose purpose in the play is only to speak these 24 lines, allow the audience to feel the literally *unnatural* character of Richard's dissolute kingship and Bolingbroke's rebellion.

In this scene, Shakespeare depends upon actor playing the Welsh Captain to unleash the transformative power of the theatre, turning the bare stage into a landscape of withered trees bloodily overlooked by a pale-faced moon. The Captain's speech is a variation on the theatrical phenomenon we saw in Northumberland's list of names at II.i.277–88: it gives the audience a sense of the way in which the events of the play extend beyond the boundaries of the stage to a populous, living world. The kind of external world suggested by the Welsh Captain is not a political one, filled with particular persons. It is, rather, a mythical world, filled with types: prophets, rich men, ruffians. The effect of constructing an idea of this mythical world is to elevate the role of King, and the act of rebellion against the King, to a symbolic level – to construe Richard's misrule and imminent downfall as both cause and symptom of a universal order turned upside down.

Act III

Act III, scene i

1–2 When Bolingbroke exits at II.iii.164–5, it is toward 'Bristow's castle, which they say is held / By Bushy, Bagot, and their complices'. An audience would have little reason to doubt this information. Bolingbroke's intelligence has been very reliable so far, and Bushy, Bagot, and Green might not be distinct enough characters so as for an audience would remember that, in II.ii it was Bushy and *Green* who headed to Bristow castle, while Bagot went to Ireland to seek out the king (II.ii.134–43). An attentive spectator might well, however, notice the discrepancy between what Bolingbroke says in II.iii and what

happens at Bristow castle in the first lines of III.i, when 'Bushy and
Green' are ordered forth. This little puzzle, which involves deciding
whether and how to make what is said on stage correspond with
what happens on stage, might be most simply solved by changing
Bolingbroke's line at II.iii.165 to 'By Bushy, Green, and their complices'.
Alternatively, one might leave Bolingbroke's line in II.iii as it is and
attempt to make the confusion 'read' in the staging of the play. A director might, that is, see the inconsistency in Bolingbroke's information as a sign that the lines of communication between Bolingbroke,
Northumberland, and Northumberland's forces are not as efficient
as they seemed to be at the end of II.i, and might thus decide to play
the multiple entrances and expository conversations of II.iii as the
frantic bustle of imminent combat rather than as Bolingbroke's clear
assumption of control in England. In such a staging, Bolingbroke's
'Bring forth these men', (III.i.1) might be performed as he strides
onto the stage, fresh from victory but still uncertain exactly who
his adversaries are; there is a pause as he identifies them, then pro-
ceeds with confident, ruthless vigour: 'Bushy and Green, I will not
vex your souls.'

A related puzzle to that of Bolingbroke's inconsistency is the
disappearance of Bagot after II.ii. In III.ii, Richard will return
from Ireland without Bagot by his side, as II.ii.140 might have led
us to expect; and he even comments upon his absence: 'Where is
the Earl of Wiltshire? Where is Bagot? / What is become of Bushy?
Where is Green?' (III.ii.122–3). An audience has a ready answer for
the questions of the second line, but not the first. One way a playing company, or an actor, might answer this question is by means
of characterization: perhaps Bagot was lying when he said he was
going to Ireland, and was always planning to desert Richard. Or,
more complexly, perhaps he hoped that his gesture toward Ireland
would encourage Bushy and Green to come along with him; when
it did not, he found that he did not have the courage to go by himself. It is also possible that even while the text does not indicate that
Bagot is on stage at this point, a production might choose to bring
him on. Bagot will reappear under somewhat surprising circumstances in IV.i, now apparently aligned with Bolingbroke (see my
commentary below). To bring him on stage at this point, a silent
and enigmatic figure (has he been captured? has he willingly joined
with Bolingbroke?) who must stand by while his former friends are

sent to execution, might be a powerful way to express the depth and complexity of the forces that are beginning to hem Richard in on every side.

3–35 Bolingbroke's indictment of Bushy and Green contains at its centre another, different kind of puzzle involving the difference between what is said on stage and what the audience sees or has seen. 'You have in manner with your sinful hours / Made a divorce betwixt his queen and him', Bolingbroke says, 'Broke the possession of a royal bed, / And stained the beauty of a fair queen's cheeks' (III.i.11–14). The suggestion of homosexuality, for which there has been no explicit evidence in the text so far, might be read retroactively as a cue for how the actor playing Richard is to perform his relationship with these 'caterpillars' in I.iv, and possibly even during their entrance in II.i – the only time the text directs the characters to be on stage together. At the same time, there is, as the Signet footnote indicates, 'no suggestion elsewhere in the play that Richard was estranged from his queen'. Quite the contrary, when in II.ii the Queen speaks of her husband's departure with affectionate sorrow, she does so to Bushy, Bagot, and Green, who seem to respond as confidants and friends.

This discrepancy between what Bolingbroke says and what we have seen on stage is easier to 'play' than the Bagot/Green discrepancy. Bolingbroke is, as the Signet footnote says, 'making a propaganda speech'. It is significant and perhaps all too predictable that Bolingbroke's first act upon returning to England and beginning his ascent to power is not only one of violence, but an act of violence framed by a rhetorical posture that is manifestly at odds with what it seeks to represent. There is a parallel with Richard here, of course, but there is also a significant difference. Bolingbroke may be as adept as his cousin at using language to manipulate events but, at least some of the time, he is cagey enough to avoid presenting his language *as* a manipulative rhetorical posture. Bolingbroke's speech at the beginning of III.i is unrhymed blank verse. This is the case with all of his language from the moment he returns to England until after he takes the crown from Richard (with the single exception of his rhymed couplet at the end of III.i). All of his speeches, that is, outside of contexts that require a ceremonial persona (the Parliament of I.i, the Lists of I.iii, once he is effectively the King after IV.i) do not _sound_ explicitly artificial no matter how artificial it might actually be. There is a pointed and significant contrast between his thirty unrhymed lines in III.i and the four lines with which Bushy and Green leave the play, a jointly created rhyme, reminiscent of the language of Richard's court, coupling _farewell_ and _hell_.

36 to the end   The final lines of this scene present yet one more puzzle, as Bolingbroke refers to an imminent fight with 'Glendower', a character to whom we have not been introduced by name (possibly he is meant to be the Welsh Captain of II.iv), and whose role in the resistance to Bolingbroke's rebellion will not be mentioned again in the play. Some editors of the play have understood discrepancies such as this, or the Bagot/Green problem, to be palimpsests: traces of unrevised work which provide evidence of multiple stages of composition. Perhaps at one point, Shakespeare had planned, or even written a speech in which Bagot explains his decision not to go to Ireland, and then decided to cut it; perhaps he had planned, or even written, some scenes with Owen Glendower and then decided that the character could be saved for a later play such as _1 Henry IV_. That Shakespeare might have subjected his play to revision, and that some evidence for revision has been preserved in the printed text, does not seem to me unlikely, and a director might certainly cut line 43 without interfering with an audience's comprehension of the narrative. At the same time, a director might also see the multiple expository puzzles of this scene as a pattern, and this pattern as characterizing the nature of Bolingbroke's rise to power and his eventual kingship: the world ruled by Bolingbroke is not only one where what is said and what happens do not always correspond, but it is also a world where we, the theatrical audience, are always a step behind, unable to determine exactly what is confusion and what is the performance of confusion. We are dependent upon the cagey, tight-lipped politician to reveal, at his discretion, the information we need in order to predict and interpret what's going to happen next.

Act III, scene ii

1–3   As at the end of Act II, the scene here is Wales. But the change of location is signaled in a different way. Whereas in II.iv, Shakespeare's audience would have had the Welsh Captain's accent to indicate a new lanscape, in III.ii Richard simply speaks the name of the castle they have come to: 'Barkloughly Castle call they this at hand?' This expository moment is followed by another: 'How brooks your Grace the air / After your late tossing on the breaking sea?' asks Aumerle. In these three lines we see another version of the deft economy with which Shakespeare is able to transform his bare stage and ask an audience to imagine a series of events that it has not seen.

4–27 One of Richard's chief objectives in this scene is to establish a connection with and claim to the land, and thus to convince his followers of the illegitimacy of Bolingbroke's claim. This speech provides the actor playing Richard not only the opportunity to relish the rhetorical flourishes with which the King curses Bolingbroke (see, for example, the vivid imagery of III.ii.14–17), but also the opportunity to physicalize those flourishes and to embody his connection with the land itself. 'Dear earth, I do salute thee with my hand', Richard says at line 6, and probably kneels down on the stage, transforming its bare boards into an expanse of fertile soil. The next five lines figure Richard as a loving mother fondling her child, and we see him caress the earth, doing it 'favors with my royal hands' (III.ii.11).

While it is unlikely to have occurred in Shakespeare's theatre, a modern playing company might cover part of its stage with a thin layer of actual dirt, some of which is perhaps arranged in a small hillock adorned with flowers, so that Richard can range about the space throughout the speech, perhaps plucking a flower at line 19 and deliberately putting it in his clothing or his hair; perhaps embracing, at line 24, the very stones he expects will take on a life of their own to protect him. Whether or not the stage on which this scene is played 'realistically' represents the earth, the speech demands of the actor a remarkable performance as he engages with something inanimate as though it were animate; and the kind of hyperbolic acting required of both actor and character as he attempts to make things other than they are has lasting repercussions for an audience's interpretation of the King's character for the rest of this scene, and indeed the rest of the play.

28–35 Two new characters are introduced in this scene: the Bishop of Carlisle and the Lord Scroop. Carlisle, when we hear him speak for the first time, is impractically verbose and self-important.

His heavily balanced, opaquely aphoristic expression of the force bestowed upon the King by the principle of divine right (III.ii.28–32) must be put into plain terms by Aumerle (III.ii.33–5), a minor character who begins to come into his own as Richard's right-hand man in this scene. Scroop, who appears later in the scene, speaks in elegant metaphors that seem calculated to allow him to avoid confronting Richard with the full weight of the bad news he has to report.

36–63 Richard's response to Aumerle's exhortation to fight encapsulates one of the most significant problems for the actor performing the role of the King and the audience's response to him. On one hand, given what we have seen and heard of Bolingbroke's progress, Richard's speech at lines 36–63 is astonishingly hyperbolic and ludicrously overconfident in its assertion that God is on the side of monarchy and that the King need do little more than show himself to the rebels in order to put rebellion down. The climactic and most dramatic image of the speech is its last, as Richard imagines an army of angels paid by God to fight on his behalf (III.ii.58–62). On the other hand, the substance of Richard's speech is entirely reasonable (however hyperbolic it might be) if one is convinced, as Richard is, of the principle of the divine right of kings: 'Not all the water in the rough rude sea / Can wash the balm off from an anointed king' (III.ii.54–5). We can assume that Shakespeare's audience would in general have had a stronger feeling than we do of the potential reality of divine right, and the powerfully heightened rhetoric of this speech is meant both to express and play upon that feeling. But as Shakespeare's representation of Bolingbroke itself demonstrates, the principle of divine right was, in the late sixteenth century, something about which it was possible to be quite sceptical; and even before a secular twenty-first-century audience, the actor playing Richard should be proficient enough at this extravagant performativity to make the spectators begin to believe what he says – both to invest in the seductive possibility that kingly power is authorized by God and to see the practical realities that complicate this possibility when, at line 63, Richard snaps out of his divinely inspired oratory to ask the approaching Salisbury when a *mortal* army will arrive to help him fight.

64–143 Richard makes himself the central focus of the first 63 lines of the scene by performing: kingship and the rhetoric of kingship become the same thing as Richard seduces himself and his auditors, on-stage and off, with visions of a power over men and nature conferred by God Himself. Over the course of the next 80 lines, Richard remains the central focus, but for an inverse or opposite reason: now his part is purely reactive as he is beset on all sides by bad news. Lines 93–103 show Richard still attempting to insist that God is on his side, but the strain circumstances have put upon his religious rhetoric is evident when, at lines 133–4, he calls upon the aid of 'Terrible hell' rather than God and an army of angels. The lines from Aumerle provide cues for the actor playing Richard to show other, physical signs of strain along the way. 'Comfort, my liege', he says twice (III ii.75, 82), perhaps hesitating as he reaches out to touch Richard's shoulder before thinking better of it. At lines 129–34, Richard misinterprets the tentative, perhaps frightened Scroop's equivocation (III.ii.128) as suggesting that Bushy, Green, and Wiltshire have *actually* 'made peace with Bolingbroke'. When Scroop clarifies that he meant to say that Richard's friends are dead, we are given no lines of reaction from Richard. Rather, Aumerle is given a line of quiet disbelief (III.ii.141), which is perhaps meant to emphasize Richard's stunned silence, and to throw into sharp relief the renewed and digressive loquacity with which the King begins to speak at line 144, once he has fully processed the news of Bolingbroke's increasing power.

144–77 In Richard's first speech in this scene, he imagines the earth's stones becoming 'armed soldiers', coming to life in his defence. Scroop's speech at lines 104–20 inverts this image, painting a picture of Richard's subjects, their voices, joints, bows, and distaffs inexorably turned against the king. In Richard's first speech in the scene, his focus is directed downward, toward the stage, as he works to connect his body to the land he plans to hold against the rebellion of Bolingbroke. In his speech at lines 144–77, Richard probably directs his focus downward once again, but the physical connection with the earth he expresses in this speech is the inverse of what it was in his first speech: there, he imagined the earth as coextensive with his flesh in the manner of a child; here, he imagines it as coextensive with his flesh insofar as he is merely dust: 'nothing can we call our own, but death / And that small model of the barren earth / Which serves as paste and cover to our bones' (III.ii.152–4).

At line 155, Richard probably sits heavily down upon the stage. This line invites his friends and followers to join him in this position, but it seems likely that they do not. As Richard abdicates the position of King for the position of storyteller, and imagines himself a historical character in his own narrative (III.ii.156–70), further and further abstracting himself from the reality of his present moment, Scroop, Aumerle, Salisbury, and Carlisle perhaps stand clustered around him, slightly embarrassed, uncertain whether to stoop to their sovereign's level, or how to help him back up to where he ought to be. Richard's injunction 'Cover your heads' at line 171 indicates that his followers are standing with their hats in their hands, as a sign of respect, attempting to maintain the appearance of ceremonial protocol in this moment of crisis. Even as Richard's storytelling and his attempt to reject ceremonial protocol dramatize an extreme form of political weakness, they also allow him to achieve a powerful connection with the theatrical audience – a connection that becomes more and more important for defining Richard's 'true' identity and power over the remainder of the play (see, especially, commentary below on V.vi). Sitting on the stage, Richard is now more on eye level with the audience that surrounds him; and in this moment, his rejection of the protocols of royal power are made in service of a radical social levelling. He seems to speak directly to the audience in the last lines of the speech: 'I live with bread like you, feel want, / Taste grief, need friends' (III.ii.175–6). These needs and desires and feelings are, Richard insists, more important than the mere title of 'king' (III ii.177). The extent to which he is able to convince the audience that this is true will largely determine the extent to which the audience favours weak Richard over powerful Bolingbroke.

178–214   The Bishop of Carlisle's second speech (III.ii.178–85) in the scene is no more lucid than his first, and it is, like the first, followed by terse, practical counsel from Aumerle (III.ii.186–7). At this point Aumerle is perhaps meant to be played as ruthlessly efficient, almost a Bolingbroke-in-training, the kind of person who could save Richard if only Richard would pay him any attention. Richard does, for a moment, heed Aumerle here, taking heart at the mention of York's army. It is now the lot of the hapless Scroop – a gift part for an actor capable of representing the discomfort of a man duty-bound to be in the middle of the most impossible situations – to tell Richard that York has gone over to Bolingbroke. The efficiency of Aumerle comes to naught, and Richard refuses to hear him any more.

215 to the end   The scene ends with a puzzling ellipsis. 'My liege, one word', Aumerle calls, perhaps hoping to offer one more piece of practical advice as an alternative to Richard's plan to 'pine away' at Flint Castle (III.ii.209). 'He does me double wrong / That wounds me with the flatteries of his tongue', Richard says, and storms off stage. It seems likely that he has hopefully misinterpreted Aumerle's intent – that Aumerle was not planning to speak 'flatteries' but policy. But Richard, in the scene's final and most devastating symmetry, is as intent on performing his own destruction as he was on performing his own power in the scene's first lines. In silencing Aumerle, Richard has recaptured, in a way, some of the theatrical power he had at the beginning of the scene; shutting out 'vain' counsel, Richard no longer has to *react*, only to act.

Act III, scene iii

1–19   Bolingbroke enters in mid conversation, and what he says gives important expository information about the state of his rebellion. Once again, the audience is reliant upon Bolingbroke for information, and half a step behind his receiving and delivering it. In this scene, Northumberland seems to have put aside for the moment the anxiety about Bolingbroke's motives, which he might have expressed in II.iii. He could be portrayed as almost obsequious in his first lines (III.iii.5–6), and servile in his actions later in the scene. It is of course entirely possible that this servility is an optimistic, calculated pose; that Northumberland is playing the role of obedient henchman in order to convince Bolingbroke that there is no need to take more than he came for.

Northumberland's omission of Richard's title, 'King', at line 6 actually could be the 'mistake' he immediately protests to York that it is. Northumberland, one of Bolingbroke's chief regional rivals, has as much interest as anyone in keeping Richard on the

throne and Bolingbroke off it; he might be genuinely mortified at
his own slip of the tongue. At the same time, a particularly sophisticated actor might represent this apparent slip as an attempt to
raise the stakes in Northumberland's continuing political poker
game with Bolingbroke; an attempt, that is, to draw out his intentions. Bolingbroke, of course, is too good a player to be drawn out.
His replies to York's vehement warnings against exceeding the
bounds of his legitimate claim on Lancaster are brilliantly equivocal. 'I … oppose not myself / Against [the heavens'] will' (III.iii.18–19)
can be understood as an orthodox affirmation of the principle of
Richard's divine right ('I am not seeking more than I should, because
that would be against the will of God'), or as a subtle assertion of his
belief in his own providential rise to power ('It is the will of God that
I take the throne').

20–9   As in II.iii, Bolingbroke is still in a somewhat precarious
position, always on the verge of being set upon by hostile forces,
never completely certain who is coming toward him. 'But who
comes here?' he asks after silencing York, and this is an echo of
his repeated question in II.iii. The difference with this scene, however, is that now no one needs to tell Bolingbroke who is approaching. He recognizes Northumberland's son and addresses him as
Northumberland addressed him in II.iii, as 'Harry'. Actors playing the roles of Bolingbroke and Harry Percy might use this brief
moment of intimate naming to convey to the audience a history of
a quickly and deeply developed bond between the two men; such
a performance of intimacy might, in turn, foreshadow the development of the men's relationship in 1 *Henry IV*, where Percy will be
discussed as a kind of surrogate son to Henry IV when the latter is
disappointed with Prince Hal.

30–70   For the next forty or so lines, Bolingbroke is absolutely
in control of the Percies, of the stage and of the audience. Harry
Percy explains Richard's whereabouts; Northumberland identifies the 'clergyman' with him as the Bishop of Carlisle and is then
dispatched to set up a parley with the King; the on stage entourage
marches at Bolingbroke's repeated command; the audience perhaps
follows Bolingbroke's gaze, or his pointing finger, as he announces
Richard's appearance on the walls and competes with its pageantry

and fanfare by means of an uncharacteristically ornate simile (III. iii.61–5). The speech that Bolingbroke gives prior to this simile, and especially lines 34–47 where he tells Northumberland what to tell Richard, is a masterpiece of manipulation worthy of Richard himself. Starting with professions of humility and submission (III. iii.34–40), Bolingbroke gradually allows himself to lose control of his imagination and his syntax, revelling in the terrible image of his own destructive power (III.iii.41–3) before contorting his sentence in such a way as to suggest, with perhaps an audible sneer, 'how far off from the mind of Bolingbroke' such violence is.

71–119 Towering above the rebels, Richard might stand for sometime 'upon the walls', peering down in imperious silence. He is waiting for someone to kneel, and when he sees that it might not happen, he breaks his silence: 'We are amazed, and thus long have we stood, / To watch the fearful bending of thy knee, / Because we thought ourself thy lawful king.' The scene becomes, in part, a contest of levels, each character trying to maintain his, or bring another character down from his. There is no stage-direction in the early texts indicating that Northumberland should kneel. If the text's silence on the matter is followed, we can see Northumberland as victorious in this first round of the contest. At the same time, Northumberland has little to gain from encouraging outright rebellion against the power of the king, and he might, having established with his initial resistance that his duty is *merely* duty, kneel for the remainder of his encounter with Richard, secure in the assumption (correct, as it turns out) that Bolingbroke will later kneel as well.

120–41 The stage in this scene must be imagined as representing a space significantly larger than itself. Richard notes at line 90 that Bolingbroke 'stands'; however, the latter seems to be far enough off that Richard does not expect him to kneel. At line 120, Richard instructs Northumberland in his reply to Bolingbroke. Again, this is an indication that Bolingbroke is meant to be understood as far enough away not to hear. At line 125, Northumberland presumably walks back to the part of the stage occupied by Bolingbroke and holds a conversation with him that is entirely separate from the lengthy conversation Richard enters into with Aumerle. At some point during Richard's subsequent long speech (III.iii.142–74),

Northumberland must re-traverse the stage, arriving at a place
where he can be addressed by Richard at line 171. This is not to say,
however, that the scene could not be performed on a small stage, or
indeed on a large stage but without the illusion of distance implicit in the text. A production that was at pains to *avoid* the illusion
of distance might well create a poetic and structural energy in the
scene which would connect it to the pageantry of I.i and I.iii. In such
a staging, where Bolingbroke could hear what Northumberland
said to Richard and Richard to Northumberland, and where both
Bolingbroke and Northumberland could hear what Richard said to
Aumerle, the emphasis would be on ritual and performance – on
the careful observation of the protocol of the parley, and on the self-
conscious self-abasement of a cornered king preparing to play his
greatest role: that of his own usurper.

142–6 Before he descends to the base court, Richard voices his
intention to give up his crown, and the speech in which he does so
is representative of the theatrically potent way in which he moves
between relinquishing and maintaining power. The first four lines
of Richard's long speech might be spoken rapidly and with a sense of
sardonic desperation. Richard's rhetorical questions and his answers
to them are split up within and across lines in such a way as to suggest both that he is quickly coming to a realization of the helpless-
ness of his position, and that he is eager to prevent anyone else from
expressing this fact. Line 144 ends in mid clause, 'Must he lose', and
is completed at the beginning of line 45, 'The name of king?' An actor
might play against the enjambment here, taking the visual cue provided by the line ending as a signal to pause, mid-breath, as Richard
prepares himself to verbalize what it is that he must lose. The first
half of line 145 is then followed by an almost flippant dismissal of the
thing he has no choice but to give up.

146–58 The character of Richard's speech changes significantly
between lines 146 and 158, which are no longer broken into pieces.
His syntax corresponds to the structure of his metre since there
are no further moments where enjambment breaks a grammatical
clause in half. The anaphora and the imagery of lines 147–51 give his
speech the feeling of an incantation and suggest that he has thought
out, in a comprehensive poetic way, what it might mean to forsake

the power of kingship. All of this is a masterly performance, and the artificiality especially of lines 147–51 is meant to indicate, as much as anything else, that Richard might be trying to convince himself of something he does not actually believe. But the performance is not necessarily any less affecting for being a performance. Nor is it accurate to say that because Richard is clearly performing at this moment, what he is giving up – and the act of doing so – is insubstantial. This is because for both Richard and the audience, Richard's histrionic and kingly personae are so deeply intertwined that *only* Richard himself can perform this ritual of discarding it.

159–74   At line 159 Richard notices that Aumerle is crying. This may be a cue for other actors in Richard's party to cry as well, and it may be meant to stand for the emotional impact Richard's performance has upon *all* the characters on-stage, including his adversaries. Through the next ten lines, Richard certainly has the opportunity to build a sense of pathos. He focuses in on Aumerle, making him a companion in something like a suicidal fantasy, imagining the two of them dying of broken hearts, their close bond being eternally memorialized for all to see in a 'pair of graves / Within the earth' (III.iii.166–7).

As moving as this fantasy might be, it also might be another of Richard's manipulations, transparent to those who watch him create it. At lines 169–70 Richard cuts short his twin-grave fantasy, seeming to notice that others on the stage are laughing at him. Perhaps he is only referring to Aumerle, and Aumerle is not laughing so much as smiling sympathetically or helplessly at Richard, who now realizes that he cannot ignore Northumberland any longer. It might be, however, that Richard's antagonists on the stage below have been observing his lengthy colloquy with Aumerle, and have begun to become impatient with it, and to show their impatience with smirks and smiles; and this smirking is perhaps what gives impetus to Richard's scornful, grim sarcasm at lines 172–3: 'Will his Majesty / Give Richard leave to live till Richard die?'. Perhaps Northumberland is briefly embarrassed, caught in his own break from decorum, and hastily makes the 'leg' to which Richard refers at line 174. If so, the lapse in decorum would seem to give Richard some pleasure: he relishes the fact that his antagonists must try as hard as possible to suppress the truth of the situation, a truth which he himself freely, insistently expresses.

175–95   Though he plans to kneel to the King, as we see at line 186, Bolingbroke seems intent on establishing a relatively level playing field first. His request, spoken through Northumberland, is that the King 'come down' off the walls. The fact that Richard sees the nature of the game Bolingbroke is playing is evident in his picking up and playing upon the words *down* and *base*. ('base court' is literally the lower courtyard, but Richard brings out the pejorative moral and class-inflected connotations of *base*.). How much Bolingbroke is interested in achieving beyond a kind of symbolic victory is unclear in the text, and it is probably at the actor's discretion how much he makes clear to the audience. Interestingly, the audience's (or reader's) uncertainty about what Bolingbroke wants – simply 'his own' or the kingdom itself – comes in large part from Richard. As soon as he sees that Bolingbroke is willing to play the game of humility – to kneel before his sovereign – Richard suggests that he is fully prepared to give Bolingbroke more than he has ever made explicit that he might want. 'I come but for mine own', Bolingbroke says at line 194, and Richard replies, surprisingly, 'Your own is yours, and I am yours, and all.' Richard's reply is perhaps a Northumberland-style attempt to raise the stakes and so cause Bolingbroke to show his hand; but the consequences are, of course, much greater for Richard, and his apparent willingness to accept these consequences is what gives him so much control at the very moment he relinquishes power.

196 to the end   Bolingbroke's reply might seem to suggest that he has not appreciated the significance of what Richard has just given him. He continues to speak in the equivocal language of an obedient subject, apparently seeking nothing more than his 'own'. But of course, Bolingbroke's refusal to discard the language of subjection is more cagey than obtuse. Richard's theatrical generosity has given Bolingbroke no choice but to speak – to make explicit – his willingness to accept what Richard has offered. But as long as Richard is on stage, Bolingbroke refuses to do this. In his final line of the scene, Bolingbroke speaks as a subject must speak to a King: 'Yea, my good Lord' (III.iii.207). As we will see in IV.i, only when Richard is off stage is Bolingbroke willing to speak as a king: 'In God's name, I'll ascend the regal throne', he says at IV.i.110. This firmness of purpose will almost immediately be thwarted by the intrusion of Richard himself into the scene, out-performing Bolingbroke and, more importantly, as here at the end of III.iii, forcing Bolingbroke to begin his reign pretending to be something he is not.

Act III, scene iv

1–28   This scene introduces a dramatic change of rhythm. It is the first time the Queen has been on stage since the first half of II.ii and that the audience has seen any action other than the gradually converging movements of the forces of Richard and Bolingbroke. Significantly, the scene itself is not concerned with naturalistic details of political and military negotiation, but rather with ornate theatrical metaphors used to express abstract thematic concerns central to the play.

The stage direction at the beginning of the scene does not specify how many female attendants enter with the Queen, but Signet's guess, 'two ladies', seems reasonable given the limitations faced by an early modern acting company. If this is indeed the case, the Queen and her entourage are in a way reflected by the Gardener and his two men when these latter enter at line 23. What is perhaps most notable about the entrance of the Gardener and his two men as they set to work is how they seem to take no notice of the Queen. On one hand, we are probably meant to imagine the stage being used to convey the illusion of space and distance: the Queen and her ladies stand in one place that is made to seem entirely separate from the 'garden' space in which the Gardener and his men work and converse. But this separation is not merely functional. It has thematic ramifications insofar as it represents the lack of contact between two social and political worlds – lofty sovereign and lowly subjects – which has implicitly been a part of Richard's reign since he scoffed at Bolingbroke's wooing of oyster wenches at I.iv.31–6.

29–71   Next to the prison scene (V.v), this scene is perhaps the most specifically localized in the play. ('What sport shall we devise *here in this garden?*' is the first line.) As a result, modern productions often add visual details that help signify the location: garden-benches, sometimes a potted tree or two, occasionally even a patch of earth or grass in which flowers or other plants can be seen to grow. It is fairly unlikely that a sixteenth-century audience would have seen such scenic details. Shakespeare's writing in this scene is scrupulous in the way it avoids requiring the actors to interact with a realistic garden. The Queen and her Ladies 'step into the shadow of these trees' at line 25, and this is probably a reference to the pillars that held up the roof above the stage. The Gardener, at his entrance, directs his men to perform some gardening work, but does so in such a way that we can imagine this work happening in a part of the garden that exists only offstage: 'Go, bind thou up young dangling apricocks' (III.iv.29); 'Go thou, and ... Cut off the heads of too fast growing sprays' (III.iv.33). At the end of the scene, the Gardener refers to a place on the stage as the site for a 'bank of rue' (III.iv.105), but since the actor must exit at this point, the actor in the Lord Chamberlain's Men probably imagined that his rue-seeds were somewhere off stage, and that he would come back later to plant them. (Modern theatre companies, which have the ability to turn off the lights at the end of a scene, sometimes have the Gardener kneel at this point and begin to mime the action of planting.)

What the early modern stage probably did require for its gardeners in this scene was costumes, and perhaps tools, that signified their occupation. Modern productions make the gardeners look like gardeners, and often also make them *sound like* gardeners by having them speak in broad working- or lower-class accents. As the first non-noble characters to appear in the entire play (with the possible exception of the Welsh Captain), the gardeners can, in their speech and their dress, introduce a significant new visual and aural element into the audience's experience. At the same time, it is worth noting that the gardeners are somewhat unusual, as non-noble characters introduced briefly and for the purpose of offering a very specific and new social perspective, in that they do not speak in prose. As much as the gardeners are meant to dramatize the gulf between nobility and commoners, their language also works to suggest that in this play's vision of medieval England, all classes are united in the attempt to give the most precise, poetic expression possible to the problems of royal power and rebellion.

The actors playing the Gardener and his men might show an awareness of the Queen's presence, and stage their ensuing conversation as an attempt to keep both a respectful and a discreet distance as they go about their work, and as they speak in metaphors that they know the Queen would not want to hear; also possible is a staging where the gardeners actually *try* to be overheard, as if unintentionally, by the Queen, so that their analogy of kingdom and garden becomes not only direct political commentary but also something like advice to Richard through the Queen. But I think the form this scene is probably supposed to take is one in which the gardeners are not aware of the Queen's presence, and where their analogies between garden and kingdom seem to arise naturally and inevitably out of their work so as to express a central 'truth' about the play, This truth is importantly independent of the rhetorical postures we get from Richard and those who must perform for him.

72 to the end   Because of their separateness from the Queen, and because of the way their political commentary develops out of the specialized vocabulary of their trade, the gardeners on one level seem to occupy the privileged position of having access to a perspective that perhaps only gardeners might be able to have. They embody the central importance of the *land* which we have heard from Gaunt, Bolingbroke, and Richard over the course of the play; and they seem acutely aware of the ramifications of Richard's and Bolingbroke's quarrels over and upon this land. In these terms, the effect of the gardeners is to call into question Richard's power by locating a critique of it in the specialized, non-political vocabulary of a certain segment of the working class.

At the same time, the gardeners are also probably meant to represent not a privileged point of view, but the point of view of all of England. The Queen is surprised by the news of Richard's deposition. She bridges the gap between herself and the gardeners in order to express this surprise, but the conversation that ensues only opens up a wider gap between her position and that of the people: 'I speak no more than everyone doth know', the Gardener says at line 91. As has happened in earlier scenes with Bushy and Bagot and Green, or with Ross and Willoughby, minor characters develop a super-reliable, representative perspective precisely because they are minor. It is unlikely that the actors playing Bushy, Bagot, and Green doubled with the Gardener and his two men. (I have a feeling that the actor cast as Mowbray was meant to reappear here in the form of the Gardener, and some modern productions cast the role with the actor who played Gaunt.). Nevertheless, the stage image of the sorrowful Queen surrounded by three well-intentioned gardeners is a powerful inversion of the stage image in I.iv, where Richard, exalting in his power, was surrounded by three 'caterpillars'.

Act IV

Act IV, scene i

1–6 The beginning of IV.i, with its ritualized accusations and throwing down of gages, is an echo of the play's opening scene. A production certainly might emphasize the parallel, perhaps by means of music, movement, and costuming; and/or by positioning Bolingbroke centrally (and/or above) so that he occupies the same space as Richard in I.i, in his role of mediator in the ensuing quarrel. The positioning of the other lords in the scene might also be symmetrical in such a way as to recall the polar oppositions of the first scene: Northumberland, an echo of John of Gaunt in his necessary but tense relationship to the supreme power in the scene, might stand at Bolingbroke's right hand. Percy, Fitzwater, Surrey, and the anonymous Lord, the appellants of this scene, take one side of the stage, while Aumerle, Carlisle, and the Abbot of Westminster take the other. Between and among them are arranged a company of Heralds and court officers. The echoes of I.i would underscore the one striking absence of Richard in this scene of pageantry and ceremony.

Richard's absence is in a way complemented by the surprising presence of Bagot, whom Bolingbroke calls onto the stage at line 1, and whom we have not seen since the end of II.ii. It is puzzling that Shakespeare uses Bagot to accuse Aumerle, and that Bagot reintroduces the Woodstock problem at this point in the play. The episode represented in this scene does occur in Holinshed, but this cannot be entirely its reason for appearing in the play: Bagot and Aumerle have, up to this point, been on the same side (Richard's), and nothing in the text has indicated a rivalry between them (though such a thing might be indicated silently by means of stage business in I.iv, the only scene where the two men appear on stage together); moreover, the issue of Woodstock's death has not been a concern of the play since Gaunt's death scene. Why does Shakespeare use this apparently irrelevant historical material to frame the more immediately urgent business of Bolingbroke's taking the throne?

I suggest that there are at least two answers to this question. First, the surprise the audience might feel at the nagging persistence of the Woodstock problem in the action of the play could be analogous to the historical experience Shakespeare is attempting to represent, where neither Richard nor Bolingbroke can ever be free of their kinsman's murder. It is an episode of violence that will not go away, that can be dredged up for reasons of personal vengeance or political expedience at both convenient and inconvenient times. Here, Bolingbroke seems to be using it as a way of neutralizing the threat of Aumerle, while Bagot seems to be using it as a way of demonstrating his newfound loyalty to Bolingbroke. Second, Bagot's somewhat surprising re-entrance is a dramatization of the suddenness and totality of Bolingbroke's power: without any preceding on-stage explanation, Bagot has avoided the fate of Bushy and Green, and come over to Bolingbroke's side. His doing so allows Bolingbroke to stage his power as dispenser of official justice and corrector of the sins of Richard's reign, before going on to announce, finally, his own ascension to the throne. As I suggested in my commentary on III.i, such an interpretation of the scene also might have an effect on the characterization of Bagot, whom we last saw in II.iii, promising to meet Richard in Ireland. An actor working with the small role of Bagot might use his actions at the beginning of IV.i as a cue to present his words at the end of II.iii as insincere, perhaps even as subterfuge.

7–30 Bagot and Aumerle now stand forth, facing one another across the stage, performing in ceremonious rhetorical terms reminiscent of I.i their accusations of treason and protestations of loyalty. Bagot's accusation rests on two specific pieces of evidence, both direct quotations from Aumerle. The first of these (IV.i.11–13) occurred before the action of the play and is therefore not something an audience can verify one way or the other. The second (IV.i.15–17) would have occurred during the action of the play, but is not something, or even a good paraphrase of something, we have heard Aumerle say during the play. The one other time Bagot and Aumerle have been on stage together in I.iv, Aumerle indicated that he was pleased with Bolingbroke's banishment, but said nothing about 'a hundred thousand crowns'. Bagot's speech in IV.i could be taken as a cue by the actor that he and Aumerle have had off stage interaction, and probably conflict, after I.iv, and that this should be conveyed here in IV.i. Alternatively, the speech could be understood as an elaborate exaggeration and distortion of what Aumerle said in I.iv, making Bagot still more emphatically a slippery character, and a marker of the transforming power of Bolingbroke.

By IV.i, Bolingbroke has become Richard's mighty opposite. The possible staging parallels between this scene and I.i and I.iii both emphasize the opposition and suggest the way in which that opposition is always on the verge of collapsing into an identity. At line 30, Bolingbroke is in the same position as Richard was in I.i and demands from Bagot *not* to take up Aumerle's gage. There is no stage direction indicating whether Bagot takes up the gage in spite of Bolingbroke's injunction, though it is possible that he does. Whether or not Bagot takes up the gage, and/or the amount of force Bolingbroke has to put into his command that Bagot not take it up, will affect the way the audience perceives Bolingbroke's authority. Is he a stark contrast to Richard, able to control his subjects with a word and allow them to get out of control (as seems to begin to happen in the frenzy of gage-throwing) only when it suits his purposes? Or is he, more like Richard, limited in his power by the unruly passions of his subjects? Already a version of the king vexed by internecine strife that we will see in 1 *Henry IV*?

31–106 It is just possible that Bolingbroke could be represented as losing control of his subjects in this scene, but not likely. He probably stops Bagot in mid-reach for Aumerle's gage, and does so with enough quiet force to keep that character silent and still for the remainder of the scene. Bagot, after all, still alive, has a lot to be thankful for. For the next 55 lines, Bolingbroke himself remains silent and still while gage after gage is thrown down by the hot-tempered lords. Modern directors staging this play often worry about the potential for laughter as the gages pile up, especially in the moments when Aumerle responds, challenging all able-bodied men to make an accusation (IV.i.57–9), and asking for 'some honest Christian' to lend him a gage so that he can accept all their challenges (IV.i.83–5). But the comedy seems, to me, entirely intentional, and a means of dramatizing Bolingbroke's absolute power. Sharing the slightly amused, bemused perspective of the audience, scoffing inwardly at the foolishness of chivalric ritual, Bolingbroke lets all of his courtiers make their allegiances perfectly clear. Then, with the same cunning we saw from Richard in I.i, he proposes a solution that he almost certainly knows will be no solution at all. As he tells the appellants that Mowbray will be called home from banishment in order to confirm or deny the truth of the accusations, the ace up

Bolingbroke's sleeve must certainly be that he already knows what he forces Carlisle to make public: that Mowbray is dead; there will be no definitive settling of the Woodstock matter. Bolingbroke's 'Sweet peace conduct his sweet soul to the bosom / Of good old Abraham' (IV.i.103–4) seems disingenuous and exaggerated to me; but it might also, of course, be performed as a banal, perfunctory piety, or even as a piety whose sincerity the on stage audience is meant to believe. In either case, Bolingbroke has no more potent rivals in England or abroad; his allies and his enemies at court have made themselves known; he can defer the dispensation of justice for as long as he finds convenient. There is nothing left to do but ascend the throne.

107–51 If the foregoing analysis of Bolingbroke's actions is correct, the entrance of York with news that Richard will yield his 'high scepter' to his newly appointed 'heir' (IV.i.109) must seem divinely, or theatrically, ordained. Everything is falling into place for Bolingbroke. It is possible that this comes as a surprise to him, and that 'In God's name, I'll ascend the royal throne' (IV.i.113) is spoken with genuine reverence for and surprise at the powers that have put him in this position. It is also possible that he is not surprised at all, that he has been fully aware that the ceremony of justice with which the scene began would end this way, and that line 113 is self-assured and almost menacing.

The Bishop of Carlisle's intervention at this point (IV.i.114–49), one of the most powerful speeches in the play, indicates that at least one person has interpreted Bolingbroke's line as more greedy than reverent. The speech is an extraordinary opportunity for the actor playing Carlisle, who has had only four previous opportunities to speak, two of which were the almost indecipherably opaque speeches in support of Richard in III.ii. Here, Carlisle is passionately, convincingly clear in his support for Richard's divine right and his indictment of the violence Bolingbroke is about to visit upon the land. As with Richard's speech at the beginning of III.ii, the actor is meant to speak with a theatrical energy that makes an audience believe in the truth of what he says. And, as with Richard's speech at the beginning of III.ii, Carlisle's speech, and the seductive point of view it espouses, is brutally deflated immediately after he stops speaking. 'Well have you argued, sir', Northumberland says, perhaps adopting the confident sneer of Bolingbroke, 'and for your pains / Of capital treason we arrest you here' (IV.i.150–1). Somewhat similar, as well, to John of Gaunt's 'This England' speech in II.i, Carlisle's speech demonstrates that in Henry's court as in Richard's, an abundance of words is frequently a sign of weakness and desperation. It is extremely significant in this regard that Northumberland, not Bolingbroke himself, replies to Carlisle.

152–3 In the earliest extant printed edition of *Richard II*, the 1597 Quarto, IV.i ends almost immediately after Northumberland's charge to the Abbot of Westminster. In that text, Northumberland tells Westminster to keep Carlisle in his custody (Signet lines 150–3), and Bolingbroke replies: 'Let it be so', and then, 'loe, on Wednesday next, / We solemnly proclaime our Coronation, / Lords be ready all.' Bolingbroke, Northumberland, and all the lords appellant exit at this point, leaving Westminster, Carlisle, and Aumerle on the stage to speak of their secret 'plot'. The lines they speak correspond to lines 320–33 in the Signet edition.

The Quarto version of IV.i represents the emptiness of chivalric ceremony and parliamentary process extremely starkly. All effective political action happens secretly and/or out of view. Bolingbroke's plans to ascend the throne have clearly been in the works off stage for some time; Aumerle, Westminster, and Carlisle speak of a subversive plot whose details we will not learn until almost the moment it is underway. The foolish wastefulness of open political ceremony and process is perhaps embodied in this scene by the pile of gages, visible on stage throughout Carlisle's speech, then perhaps sheepishly and hastily collected by their owners on their way off the stage.

154–61 The view of political process given by the Signet's longer version of IV.i. – a version based, as is standard modern editorial practice, on the 1623 Folio text – is not necessarily more optimistic than that given in Q 1597. The secrecy of Bolingbroke's machinations in the first 100 lines, and of Carlisle, Westminster, and Aumerle's in the last 15, is part of both versions; in the longer version it is still unclear when and how the gages might be removed from the stage in a way that is not slightly cumbersome or silly. Nevertheless, the scene as it exists in the Folio and in most modern editions does make the transfer of power from Richard to Bolingbroke a partly public matter. Even though the scene consists almost entirely of a conversation between Bolingbroke and Richard, they are surrounded throughout by the lords appellant, Northumberland, and the clergymen, who are a representative cross-section of the kingdom's power structure. This requires of Bolingbroke a different kind of performance from the one with which he began the scene. He must seem reluctant to wield the power that is being given to him. Richard, too, is required to give a different kind of performance at this point – one of weakness rather than strength – but it is a performance he has to a certain extent been preparing for throughout the play. For this reason, he can be said to triumph over Bolingbroke in spite of his deposition.

162–200 Richard performs his subjection to Bolingbroke as a game, and in this game he usually takes the lead. 'Here, cousin, seize the crown', he says at line 181, and then complicates his apparent generosity: 'Here, cousin, / On this side my hand, and on that side yours' (IV.i.181–2). The repetition of 'Here, cousin' suggests a deliberately naïve, jangling tone, as Richard goads his usurper with his refusal to take the moment of deposition seriously, and also refuses to let it happen immediately. Bolingbroke's very short lines through this part of the scene (IV.i.189, 193, 199) suggest a watchful impatience. He is aware of the need to humour Richard, but eager to insist that what was decided off stage is not undone here in public view. 'Are you contented to resign the crown?' he asks, surprisingly directly at line 199. Richard takes advantage of Bolingbroke's candour to tease him with four infuriating monosyllables: 'Ay', perhaps sighed wistfully and regretfully; 'no', spoken suddenly and with a teasing smile as Richard realizes that Bolingbroke's question in this public forum gives him a small amount of space to change his mind; 'no', more emphatically now, watching for a flicker of panic in Bolingbroke's eyes; 'ay', resigned and almost impatient, or at least unconcerned, now suggesting that Richard has more important things to worry about than a petty circle of metal.

201–21 In the lines that follow from these four monosyllables, Richard rhetorically adopts, or co-opts, Bolingbroke's power, and usurps himself: 'With *mine own* hands I give away the crown' (IV.i.207). With its incantatory tone, and its premeditated, artificial structure, Richard's speech at lines 200–21 is an echo of his speech at III.iii.142–74. No longer able to derive power from the ceremony of kingship, Richard creates a ceremony out of *abandoning* kingship. Even as the artificiality of the speech insists upon the

seriousness of this moment of abdication, Richard is equally willing
to suggest that what he is doing has no importance at all because
he, unlike Bolingbroke, has recognized the true meaninglessness
of royal power. 'What more remains?' at line 221 almost mimics
Bolingbroke's ability to move rapidly from one thing to another, and
suggests a casual acceptance of his fate, as though it were merely a
small administrative matter. Richard's vacillation between these
two tonal extremes might be seen to put Bolingbroke off balance.
Bolingbroke responds, characteristically, with silence: he does not
speak at all between lines 200 and 267.

221–74   As Bolingbroke temporarily withdraws, at least verbally,
from the scene, Northumberland takes a more prominent role, insisting four times over the next 50 lines (IV.i.221–6, 242, 252, 268) that
Richard 'read o'er' the articles of deposition written up against him.
As always, there are at least two ways of imagining the character of
Northumberland here. On one hand, he might be playing the role
of Bolingbroke's henchman, doing some of the usurper's dirty work
in order to make the process seem more legitimate. On the other,
he might be seen as insisting upon the reading of the articles out of
self-interest. If Richard's deposition seems to have been arrived at by
due legal process, Northumberland can feel that he has saved face
somewhat, that he has not been deceived by Bolingbroke, and that
Bolingbroke will, as king, be held to the same rigour of law to which
he is currently holding Richard. In either case, Northumberland
does not get what he wants: Richard never reads the articles, and
Northumberland is made to look like the parrot of a legal process
incommensurate to the grandeur of kingship. The words that depose
Richard come from no one but himself.

275–303   Richard is a performer from the beginning of the play to
the end, but the audience for his performances gradually shifts. At
the moment of his deposition, he is performing almost exclusively
for himself. In I.i, I.iii, and II.i, Richard performs for his courtly
audience, and through them the theatrical audience, in an explicit
way. He stages, and revels in, his power. In Act III, especially in III.
ii, the focus of his performance turns from outward to downward:
he is still performing for us, and to a slightly lesser extent for the
on stage audience of his supporters, but what he performs is the

imaginative experience of his own disappearance into the earth. In Act IV, Richard's focus is not outward or downward so much as inward. At lines 242–3, he says that his eyes are too full of tears to allow him to read the articles of deposition, but he can nevertheless 'turn mine eyes upon myself' and 'find myself a traitor with the rest' (IV.i.246–7). At lines 259–60, he imagines himself a 'mockery king of snow, / Standing before the sun of Bolingbroke', but it is not this sun that causes him to melt away – it is, rather, *himself* (IV.i.261). And at line 268, he requests a looking glass, delivered to him at line 274, so that he can 'see the very book indeed / Where all my sins are writ, and that's myself' (IV.i.273–4).

The actor playing Richard might achieve this inward focus by refusing to look at anyone, on stage or off, throughout the scene. He takes control of the audience by denying them access to his eyes. Alternatively, he might look exclusively and steadily at the audience, suggesting that he is reflected in them, and thus seducing them into complicity with his mode of performance as opposed to Bolingbroke's. The one point at which Richard *must* break focus with everyone around him is the extraordinary moment with the mirror – an object he imbues with his 'substance' (IV.i.298) only to shatter it on the stage floor and thus render it utterly inaccessible. What lies inside Richard, what gives him the power to perform his own usurpation and to find himself 'greater than a king' remains forever hidden from view, perhaps reflected obliquely and sporadically in pieces of those surrounding him, who are reflected in the slivers of broken glass.

304–17 Richard's taunting wordplay in his last few lines in the scene (see IV.i.304–15) is, like his wordplay when he fights with Gaunt in II.i, somewhat strained. His jaunty, grating tone suggests that he is masking his despair. But Richard has won a kind of victory: he has made Bolingbroke say what he wants, and he has given it to him, all the while creating a rhetorical space for himself in which he is entirely unknowable to those around him. When he asks for Bolingbroke to 'give me leave to go…Whither you will, so I were from your sights' (IV.i.312–4), he is asking for something that he knows he has already achieved. Richard wins a theatrical victory here as well. A broken mirror is a messy prop. It is possible, even likely, that on Shakespeare's stage the mirror was broken in an upstage space over which a curtain could be drawn at the end of the scene to allow for easy clean-up. But a mirror broken at centre-stage, a piece of glass whose difficult materiality had to be dealt with at the end of the scene, might have nicely embodied or literalized what Richard achieves in this scene. If the pieces are picked up at the end of the scene by Bolingbroke's lords, or by the clergymen, or even by Northumberland and Bolingbroke themselves, the process would slow the movement toward 'Wednesday next' and the coronation. The physical requirements of the theatre (the stage must be cleared) would demand that we pay attention to what Bolingbroke has caused violently to be broken apart, and to the fact that it falls to his reign to pick up the pieces. Of course, the pieces might also be left to glint and shimmer on the stage, in which case they are a reminder of Richard's shattered self, haunting the land (the stage) that Bolingbroke took from him. In either case, the broken mirror would have an ongoing, active life among the bodies of the actors. Whether they are being picked up or trod underfoot, shards of glass must be treated warily because they are dangerous and sharp.

318 to the end   The Quarto version of IV.i makes the final moment of plotting between Aumerle and the clergymen seem hasty and expedient, a quickly conceived rebellion born out of Aumerle's resentment of his recent public harassment at the hands of Bolingbroke's supporters. In the Folio version of the scene, Aumerle might still direct the indignation of his final lines at the memories of his recent treatment, but the intervening action will make the impetus for the plot seem to come more from the Bishop of Carlisle, the play's spokesman for the principle of divine right. Speaking a rhymed couplet that has the feeling of both a proverb and a prophecy, the Bishop demonstrates an awareness of the consequences of Bolingbroke's rebellion that both depends upon and is larger than a belief in the sanctity of divine right. The Abbot of Westminster seems to fall somewhere between the voice of Aumerle and the voice of Carlisle in this scene. Presumably, because he is a clergyman, he shares Carlisle's views on the matter, but his expression of concern is nowhere near so lofty; it is, in fact, rather flip: 'Come home with me to supper: I will lay / A plot shall show us all a merry day' (IV.i.332–3). The casual sound of the rhyme, and the triviality of the word *merry* suggests an overconfidence in the simplicity of the steps necessary to launch an insurgency against Bolingbroke. This overconfidence proves to be wantonly misplaced later in Act V when Aumerle, acting on its cue, is carelessly caught red-handed and brings everyone down with him.

Act V

Act V, scene i

1–15 This is the first scene in which the King and Queen actually speak to one another. In the only other scene where the text indicates that they are meant to be on stage together (II.i), the Queen's only line is directed to Gaunt. Thus, the actors must take this opportunity to give the audience a convincing sense of a marital relationship whose character has not been indicated directly at any other point in the play.

While the Queen's language as she speaks about Richard is clearly the poetic language of love (see, for example, 'my fair rose' at line 8, and 'true-love tears' at line 10), actors who seek historical context with which to ground the interpretation and staging of this relationship will be frustrated. Historically, Richard was known to have a deeply affectionate relationship with his first wife, Anne of Bohemia, whom he married in 1383 when he was 15 and she was 16. When Anne died of the plague in 1394, Richard was stricken with grief and had Sheen Palace, where she died, destroyed. Historically, the Queen of Shakespeare's play would have to be Richard's second wife, Isabelle of France, whom Richard married in 1396, when Isabelle was eight years old. This second marriage was chiefly a political manoeuvre, made in the interest of bringing to an end years of enmity with the French; Shakespeare's representation of the royal marriage in this play seems to suggest a level of affection and intimacy similar to that associated with Richard's marriage to Anne. Interestingly, the boy actor who played the Queen in the original production of this play would probably have been near the same age as the historical Queen Isabelle during the action of the play (11 or 12), even though he is called upon to act the role of a significantly more mature woman.

16–50 The character of the Queen is never given a proper name, not in the speech headings and not in the dialogue. (There is no list of dramatis personae in any of the early texts.) This odd fact can help us to understand Shakespeare's particularly flagrant historical distortions, as well as the demands the role of Queen makes upon an actor. Shakespeare does not use the Queen to represent in any realistic way the effects of politics upon domestic life. This is more the function of the Duchess of Gloucester, who discusses the empty house to which she will return at the end of I.ii, and of the Duchess of York as we will see in V.ii and V.iii. Rather, he uses the Queen to convey a sense – not necessarily completely reliable, but certainly vivid and compelling – that Richard's problems are archetypal. The poetry of the Queen's scenes intertwines with the poetry of Richard's scenes and in so doing locates the figure of the King within a complex pattern of elevated imagery. Thus her first speech in this scene discusses Richard's progress to 'Julius Caesar's ill erected Tower' (V.i.3), the 'model where old Troy did stand' (V.i.11), and echoes Richard's speeches in III.ii concerning the 'rebellious earth' (V.i.6). To the Queen, the deposition of Richard is an inversion of the natural order of things (V.i.32–5). Like Richard, who expresses rueful disbelief that he has been deposed before he 'shook off the regal thoughts / Wherewith I reigned' (IV.i.163–4), the Queen wonders if Bolingbroke has 'Deposed thine intellect' (V.i.28). For both, kingship is far more than a mere crown, it is a state of mind.

The kind of acting called for with the character of the Queen is perhaps an understated, surprised sorrow: she is meant, I think, to reflect and emphasize the numbness Richard might feel after his final encounter with Bolingbroke. At the same time, the Queen's poetic rhetoric does contain the material for something other than numbness. It does have the potential to provide Richard with an alternative mode of response to his deposition: rage and rebellion rather than capitulation and sorrow. The gradual diminution of imagery from 'model where old Troy did stand' to 'triumph is become an alehouse guest' as the Queen addresses the Tower of London (V.i.11–15), and her surprise that Richard is content to 'fawn on rage with *base* humility' (V.i.33) could be performed as increasingly indignant and vehement. In such a reading of the Queen, she would be less a reflection of Richard and more a counterpoint to him. Richard also wants to find a response to his plight other than numb sorrow, but it is not one of rage and indignation; rather, he longs for a metamorphosis into a mystical, pastoral, eternal existence, where he is the subject of a 'lamentable tale' told 'In winter's tedious nights ... by the fire / With good old folks' (V.i.40–5).

51–70   As Richard and his Queen express poetic, unreal alternative ways of imagining what is happening to the King, Northumberland enters with a real change of plan: Bolingbroke has decided that Richard must be taken to Pomfret Castle in the north of England, rather than to the Tower of London. Richard probably realizes that this relocation, from the centre of the kingdom to a remote fortress, amounts to a death sentence, and this is perhaps why he gains the strength to lash out one final time. As in the deposition scene, Northumberland, acting as Bolingbroke's instrument, bears the brunt of Richard's wrath. Clearly committed though he is to carrying out Bolingbroke's plans, Northumberland's delivery of lines 69–70 could nevertheless suggest a troubled view of what he has got himself into. The play is full of curses and dire prophecies such as the one Richard makes against Northumberland in this scene (V.i.55–68): there is Mowbray's in I.iii, Gaunt's in II.i, Richard's in III.ii, and Carlisle's in IV.i. All of these curses are simply and easily shrugged off by the men at whom they are directed, and there is no reason to think this scene should be any different. Northumberland's 'My guilt be on my head, and there an end' could be the terse impatience of a victor who has no interest in the plaints of the vanquished.

At the same time, what Richard says of Northumberland turns out to be exactly true in the *Henry IV* plays: Northumberland rebels against Bolingbroke and brings about the destruction of his own family. A sixteenth-century audience, familiar with the history of Henry IV's reign, would have seen the irony in Northumberland's quick dismissal of Richard's words; the Northumberland actor might have even played to this irony, giving the sense that Northumberland is on some level aware of the doomed future he cannot avoid. Twenty-first-century audiences and actors also have access to this historical irony; but perhaps even more importantly, they have access to a theatrical irony that would have been unavailable to actors and audiences of the first performances of *Richard II*: we know, as actors and audiences in 1596 might not have, that Shakespeare went on to write the story of Northumberland's rebellion against Henry IV, and we might even recall that in a later play he would have characters allude to the speech Richard makes here (see 2 *Henry IV*, III.ii.70–7).

71 to the end   Whether Northumberland speaks his lines with the brusque efficiency that characterizes Bolingbroke's power, or with a burgeoning awareness of the consequences of his actions, he does not speak again for the rest of the scene. He becomes, like the theatrical audience, a spectator to the ornate poetic leave-taking between Richard and his Queen. Northumberland's role as spectator is emphasized by the fact that Richard and the Queen repeatedly address him over the course of the scene's final 30 lines, but do not allow him to respond. 'Part us, Northumberland', Richard commands at line 76, returning to the rhetorical tactic he used in the deposition scene, taking an active part in his own destruction.

After Richard's speech, at line 80, Northumberland perhaps comes forward and begins to move Richard away from the Queen. 'And must we be divided? Must we part?', the Queen asks, presumably addressing, imploring Northumberland, and perhaps taking a step or two toward Richard. But it is not Northumberland who responds with the rhetoric of necessity. Rather, it is Richard: 'Ay, hand from hand, my love, and heart from heart' (V.i.82). 'Banish us both, and send the king with me', the Queen now says, obviously addressing Northumberland. Again, perversely, it is Richard who replies, 'That were some love, but little policy', usurping Northumberland's authority to govern the structure of their parting. 'Then whither he goes, thither let me go', the Queen says, again addressing Northumberland as though he, not Richard, had just spoken. She has perhaps by this point caught up to the two men, so that Richard, in spite of all his insistence that they must be separated, is now able to embrace her as he says, 'So two together weeping make one woe' (V.i.86). At the end of this speech, Richard is perhaps deliberately cruel to his wife, trying to force her away from him: 'Go, count thy way with sighs, I mine with groans' (V.i.89), and the Queen perhaps begins to take slow, deliberate steps back across the stage, away from her husband. The intertwined poetic speech of these two lovers, as they explore the arithmetic of sorrow – where one is divided in two and two struggle to remain one – completely marginalizes the silent Northumberland. At lines 91–6, Richard is able to go against his own order in line 89 and approach the Queen again, kissing her once more before saying they must 'dumbly part'. The sonic unity of the couplets Richard and his Queen create and share mimics and embodies poetically their separateness from all eyes – those of Northumberland and of the audience; and the couplets, two lines becoming a single sonic unit, express a unity of thought and desire that works to counteract any amount of distance. Perhaps the final four lines of the scene are spoken while the two characters are at opposite corners of the stage.

Act V, scene ii

1–40   In a play replete with images and instances of doubleness and mirroring, the end of V.i and the beginning of V.ii constitute one of the most elaborate and ornate examples of poetic reflection. At the end of V.i, a loving married couple exits separately, their desire to keep talking transformed, of forced necessity, into the silence of sorrow (V.i.101–2). At the beginning of V.ii, a loving married couple enters together, the Duchess imploring her husband to continue speaking after sorrow ('weeping') caused him to 'break the story off' (V.ii.2). The poetry of the end of V.i works to make the relationship between Richard and his Queen almost untheatrical: their couplets serve to remove Northumberland from the scene almost entirely, and the audience sees its own distance from the intimately sorrowing lovers reflected in him. By contrast, the story York tells the Duchess serves an expository function for the audience – narrating an episode we would not know about otherwise – and it involves both a theatrical scenario (Bolingbroke's triumphant entrance into London) and a powerful theatrical metaphor (Richard as a poor actor following the 'well-graced actor' Bolingbroke, V.ii.23–40).

Between the end of V.i and the beginning of V.ii occurs a spectacular event – Bolingbroke's triumphant march into London with Richard captive – of which the audience is unaware until York narrates it. Instead of dramatizing this highly theatrical event, Shakespeare gives us two parallel instances of untheatrical sorrow: the movement of Richard and his Queen toward silence and invisibility at the end of V.i, and York's inability to speak at the beginning of V.ii. Gradually, in his conversation with the Duchess in V.ii, York overcomes his sorrow and finds a way to describe what we have not seen (Richard's humiliation) in theatrical terms. In arriving at these theatrical terms, York arrives at a way of understanding Bolingbroke's power as legitimate: 'To Bolingbroke are we sworn subjects now, / Whose state and honor I for aye allow' (V.ii.39–40). York's compassion for Richard's plight is resigned and practical: he knows he does not have the strength to challenge Bolingbroke's power. It is significant that the Duchess does not reply to York's story. Possibly she is simply unable to because of Aumerle's entrance; possibly she shows silent but visible disapproval of York's defeatist attitude and in this way becomes an inverse echo of Richard's more vocally resistant Queen at the beginning of V.i.

41–5 As the Duchess announces the arrival of Aumerle, York gives us further information we would not have otherwise; that, since the dispute in Parliament (IV.i), Aumerle has been demoted from the rank of Duke, left only with the title Earl of Rutland. Bolingbroke, returning to England to reclaim his lost title, has stripped his enemies of theirs. What is more, York is now 'in Parliament pledge' for his son's loyalty, a kind of political hostage. The fact that Shakespeare chooses to elide the sequence of events leading to Aumerle's demotion, as well as Bolingbroke's entrance into London, and present them in the form of expository speeches, suggests that he is attempting to emphasize the speed with which Bolingbroke works: the audience is once again in the position of catching up to crucial events.

46–72 Aumerle's attitude when he enters is studiedly nonchalant, perhaps even sullen. It might be possible to play him in this scene as a petulant youth expressing his irritation at his recent demotion by responding disinterestedly to his parents' questions. A spectator who is not fluent in the history of Richard's reign might be as innocent as York is of where the scene is headed for the first ten or so lines of Aumerle's time on stage. The Signet editor suggests that when York asks about the 'news from Oxford' Aumerle might 'give a start', but this does not seem to me to be necessary. Aumerle's next two lines (V.ii.53, 55) suggest continued nonchalance, and perhaps he is even in the midst of crossing the stage to exit. Only at the end of line 56, after York notices a 'seal' hanging in his son's jacket, is it necessary for Aumerle to react: 'Yet lookst thou pale?' York asks, and the audience, recollecting the plot alluded to at the end of IV.i, will begin to have a dramatically ironic view of the unfolding action, waiting in suspense for the moment York learns what we already know.

Lines 58–71, as York and his son struggle over the concealed 'writing' are open to a variety of tonal interpretations. On one hand, it might be played with a crescendoing intensity as both York and the Duchess come to realize that their son is involved in and attempting to conceal something very serious. On the other hand, the lines might be played comically at first, with Aumerle attempting to laugh off his father's insistence and the Duchess deflating York's initial expression of 'fear' (V.ii.64) by suggesting a trivial explanation for her son's behaviour: he's borrowed money so that he can look nice at the Oxford jousts (V.ii.64–5). This latter interpretation seems preferable to me, as it would allow for a dramatic shift in tone at lines 70–1, and for a particularly theatrical violence in realizing the stage direction, 'He plucks it out of his bosom'. This violence would feed the energy of York's exclamation 'Treason, foul treason, villain, traitor, slave!' (V.ii.72) and make it terrifying enough that Aumerle's almost complete silence (except at V.ii.82–3) for the remainder of the scene is entirely understandable.

73 to the end   After York discovers Aumerle's treasonous intentions, the scene wavers between high political drama and domestic farce. The seriousness of the situation is dramatized by Aumerle's silence, and also the one moment where he speaks and admits that what he has done 'is no more / Than my poor life must answer' (V.ii.82–3). The vigour with which the Duchess opposes her husband's plans to expose Aumerle's plot demonstrates that she knows what punishment lies in store for her son if York goes to Bolingbroke. As well, this scene echoes I.ii, where a different Duchess (perhaps played by the same actor or actress?) pleaded with a powerful man to take blood-relations into consideration as he set out on a course of political action. In the earlier scene the blood relative, Woodstock, was of course already dead; in this way, the echo between the scenes perhaps ominously doubles Aumerle and Woodstock, and underscores the dangers of disloyalty to a king, no matter who your relatives are.

At the same time, York's repeated calling for his boots (V.ii.77, 84, 87); the Duchess's threatening of the servant with the boots (V.ii.85); York's exit line, 'Make way, unruly woman' (V.ii.110); the Duchess's hasty claim that she can 'ride as fast as York' (V.ii.115); and even Aumerle's 'amazed' (V.ii.85) silence can all work to reduce the stakes of Aumerle's transgression to the level of a family squabble. Mum and Dad fight about the son's punishment and the servant gets caught in the middle. This is not to suggest that the scene or the comic element in it is mere 'comic relief'. To this point we have a still-equivocal view of the way Bolingbroke will wield power in his reign. He executes Bushy and Green, but spares Bagot; he toys with the gage-throwing courtiers in IV.i, letting their exposed loyalties hold them in a state of suspended action. The tension between comedy and fear in this scene is a result of an uncertainty about what the consequences will actually *be* for Aumerle, and this uncertainty is something Shakespeare has given the actor playing Bolingbroke an opportunity to create and cultivate.

Act V, scene iii

1–23 The scene opens with Bolingbroke wrestling with the same problem York wrestled with in the previous scene: the errors of a misguided son. Bolingbroke here refers to Prince Hal, who nowhere appears in this play but will become the central focus of all three history plays that follow it (*1 Henry IV*, *2 Henry IV*, and *Henry V*). When Bolingbroke asks about Hal's whereabouts, the response comes from Harry Percy, now more than at any other time in the play a surrogate son to Bolingbroke. It is within the power of the actor playing Percy to make the audience feel either sympathetic for Hal's behaviour (if Percy seems overly scornful or obsequious in his answer), or concerned about it (if he seems somewhat surprised, imagining the fate of England under such a king).

A modern audience, aware of the fact that the next three history plays trace Hal's development from wastrel to king, might be inclined to take a lenient attitude toward the behaviour described by Bolingbroke, and to see Hotspur's lines as indicative of doomed ambition. A sixteenth-century audience, familiar with the folk/historical tradition of stories about Henry V might have interpreted the scene and the characters in the same way. It is also important that Bolingbroke does not come down entirely on the side of Percy. He concludes their discussion of Hal on a note of indulgence and suspended judgment (V.iii.20–2) that perhaps shows the same relaxed watchfulness as his circumspect handling of the gage-throwing in

IV.i. This indulgence sets the stage for Bolingbroke's reaction to what happens next.

24–44   The York family begins to burst into the scene, bringing the world of frantic domestic farce with them. The fact that Aumerle, who left after his father in V.ii, arrives before him here might be played for laughs; Aumerle, entering 'amazed' might also indicate extreme relief upon seeing that his father is not yet there. The indulgent attitude suggested by Bolingbroke's discussion of Prince Hal is demonstrated here: Aumerle becomes for the space of the scene another of Bolingbroke's surrogate sons, a young man whose 'intended' fault can be forgiven before it is 'committed' (V.iii.32). Fully aware, from the events of IV.i, of Aumerle's potential for trouble, Bolingbroke demonstrates a confident playfulness, and perhaps an amused curiosity as Aumerle kneels, rises again, and locks the door. Maintaining this air of calm and slightly comic awareness will allow the actor playing Bolingbroke to change his aspect with frightening suddenness when York begins to pound at the door (V.iii.38). The Signet editor suggests that Bolingbroke 'Draws his sword' as he says 'I'll make thee safe', but this does not seem to me entirely necessary. Throughout the play Bolingbroke develops his power by keeping the full expression of its potential force hidden from view; it is unlikely, or at least not certain, that York's sudden, loud arrival would cause Bolingbroke to panic and summarily kill Aumerle. More in keeping with what we have seen so far would be for Bolingbroke's face and body to take on a perceptible steely purposefulness, making it extremely clear to Aumerle that he is in imminent danger of suffering at the new king's 'revengeful hand'.

45–72   York's entrance provides the opportunity for more comedy. 'What is the matter, uncle? Speak', Bolingbroke exhorts at line 45. Then perhaps he must wait a considerable beat while the old man, who has been riding as hard as he was able, catches his breath. Again, this moment of comedy is effective mainly because it sets up a tonal shift: the audience, like Aumerle, must watch in anxious suspense as Bolingbroke silently reads over the paper York has produced. Bolingbroke has, of course, as Aumerle reminds him (V.iii.50–2), promised to pardon Aumerle if his fault was intended, not committed, but when the document has been read and the announcement of pardon comes, Bolingbroke gives a new reason: 'thy abundant goodness', he tells York, 'shall excuse / This deadly blot in thy digressing son' (V.iii.65). It is possible that Bolingbroke speaks these lines for Aumerle's sake, hoping to flatter York into sharing his indulgence for youthful spirit similar to Bolingbroke's own. It is also possible that Bolingbroke does not consider a signed document of conspiracy merely an *intended* fault, but rather a fault committed, and that his indulgence of Aumerle cools rapidly over the course of this speech, making him have to work hard to find a reason to keep his promise, and to remain unconvinced by York's arguments about the dangers of pardoning vice at lines 66–72.

73 to the end   Perhaps there is a pregnant pause after York's couplet at lines 71–2 and perhaps Bolingbroke, positioned between the two men, seems seriously to be considering whether Aumerle's fault is one that can be pardoned without compromising the authority of his incipient regime. Into this tense silence cuts the 'shrill voice' of the Duchess, and this probably provides another moment of comedy, especially if York reacts with bewildered frustration. Bolingbroke's line, 'Our scene is alt'red from a serious thing' (V.iii.79) is probably meant to be directed outwardly to the audience; it is an explicit acknowledgment of their laughter and the way the squabbles of the York family have subsumed the serious political element of the scene. When Bolingbroke refers to Aumerle as 'My dangerous cousin' (V.iii.80), he probably puts ironic emphasis on the adjectives, making clear that he no longer has any intention of punishing the young man – if, indeed, he ever did. The remainder of the scene, after the Duchess enters, is a comic echo of the gage-throwing in IV.i: each of the three disputants, Aumerle, his father, and his mother, performs the ceremonial act of kneeling before the sovereign, each with a different purpose. Throughout, Bolingbroke never gives a specific sense of what he considers to be the merits of each particular kneeler's case, but allows each of them – and especially the Duchess at this point – to adopt an elaborate rhetorical posture while the King maintains a powerful posture of suspended judgment, repeating only a few terse phrases: 'Good aunt, stand up' (V.iii.109, 128) and 'I pardon him' (V.iii.130, 135). In his way, the scene is also an echo of I.i and I.iii, and Bolingbroke an echo of the earlier Richard: the king's power lies largely in silence, and economy of gesture.

After all the kneeling is done, and the suits are granted, and the three Yorks get back on their feet, there is perhaps another pregnant pause as Bolingbroke considers whether or not to say something explicit about Aumerle's 'fault'. However, he does not. He almost goes out of his way *not* to look at Aumerle, thus keeping him uncertain about how much guilt he will share even as he is free of punishment, Bolingbroke announces that the rest of the traitors 'shall not live within this world' (V.iii.141). Only in his final two lines in the scene does Bolingbroke address Aumerle directly. This is really the first time he has done so since York's entrance. What he says, 'prove you true', might be spoken in a pleasant fatherly tone, but certainly carries the hint of a threat. Aumerle has perhaps fared worse than he could have expected: his pardon has come at the expense of the lives of his friends and allies. His pardon makes him a lonely survivor, ever after isolated in Bolingbroke's watchful eye. It is significant that Aumerle has nothing to say as the characters leave the stage.

Act V, scene iv

1 to the end   As we have seen particularly vividly in IV.i and V.iii, Bolingbroke is very good at not stating his intentions, either directly or indirectly, when it suits his purposes. His ability to keep his opponents guessing is what allows him to position himself perfectly to take advantage of their weaknesses. This scene is a remarkable dramatization of this aspect of Bolingbroke's power, as it extends the reach of that power to the audience. In V.iv, we get a semi-direct expression of Bolingbroke's desire to be rid of the 'living fear' of the imprisoned Richard II. However, we get it second-hand, through Sir Pierce Exton who, narrating his conversation with Bolingbroke to the anonymous 'Man', must give a concrete meaning to the words of that conversation which Bolingbroke refused to give. While an audience might certainly have every reason to believe that Bolingbroke wants Richard dead, it might also be possible to play the role of Exton as a bloodthirsty freelance killer, more than willing to give a violent interpretation to Bolingbroke's equivocations.

Although the stage direction names Exton, neither he nor his anonymous interlocutor speaks his name in the scene. An audience familiar with Holinshed, or reading a playbill in the modern theatre, might have access to Exton's name. But Shakespeare could certainly have named him if he wanted to, and anonymity seems a deliberate and important concern of the scene. After a scene in which, by means of Aumerle's carelessness, all of Bolingbroke's enemies and political assassins become known to him by name, we get a scene where unnamed characters we have never seen before appear in order to announce their intention to assassinate the former king. In this way Bolingbroke might come to seem almost omnipotent, served by an army of identity-less men whose sole purpose is to put his words into action. Of course it is quite likely that Exton and his Man are not precisely characters we've never seen before. An early modern playing company probably would have wanted a relatively good actor for the crucial role of Richard's killer, and it is unlikely that a relatively good actor would be given *only* this role. Perhaps Exton was played by the same actor who played Mowbray, and perhaps that actor's unnamed reappearance here gives the audience a slight thrill of eerie recognition – a feeling that Richard's unreasonable fear that Mowbray and Bolingbroke would conspire together abroad (I.iii.178–90) has, at least in terms of a theatrical metaphor, proved to be justified.

Act V, scene v

1–41 Richard's 66 line speech at the beginning of this scene marks the first time in the entire play that he or anyone else has been alone on the stage. In a play that equates political power with acting and performance, such solitude is perhaps the ultimate demonstration of weakness. No one is looking at Richard and so he becomes, as he says at line 40, 'nothing'. But of course someone *is* looking at Richard – a whole crowd, in fact: the theatrical audience. And since Richard is the only one on stage, this is the first time in the play that he does not have to compete for the theatrical audience's attention. Unkinged though he may be, he now has a crowd of willing subjects before him and so, in a paradox typical of how the play works, Richard is able to be most powerful at the precise moment when circumstances suggest he should be least powerful.

The soliloquy demands a virtuoso performance by the actor playing Richard. The dense and difficult metaphors of the first 41 lines establish the former King as a self-conscious poet, one whose concerns are no longer with the material trappings of power, but rather with that which transcends all material things: the action of his own mind. The difficulty of the poetry is meant to convince the audience that Richard's final turn inward is a turn toward the heart of the play. There is no difference between beggars and kings, Richard tells us; the many parts a man might play inevitably amount to 'nothing', and what happens in the theatre – be it the theatre of monarchy, the stage of the world, or the commercial theatre itself – is trivial, meaningless compared to that which cannot be seen.

41–9   The moment Richard has committed himself and the audience to this point of view, the machinery of the theatre ostentatiously intervenes to become the basis for the King's continuing meditation on his own nothingness: '*The music plays*', according to a stage direction. At what point does the music begin? The variations among different texts of the play make this simple question difficult to answer: the Signet edition inserts the stage direction after 'With being nothing', but the Quarto text on which the Signet is based prints the stage direction next to 'Music do I hear'. The Folio text prints '*Musick*' in the margin next to the line 'And straight am nothing. But what ere I am' (Signet edition line 38), suggesting that the music plays for some time before Richard acknowledges it. Who plays the music? What does it sound like? Does it, at line 61, obediently cease at Richard's command, does it fade away gradually, or does it actually get louder, as if to mock Richard? These are all very practical theatrical questions, and any combination of possible answers has significant and immediate ramifications for how we respond to and interpret Richard's plight and what he says about it.

If, to take just one small example, the music is made to sound like the accompaniment to revelry elsewhere in Pomfret Castle – played out of time, perhaps, because played drunkenly – the audience is invited to see Richard's predicament from a broader perspective: life goes on outside his prison cell, indifferent to his solitude, and the connection he forces between the music outside and the music within himself seems like a poetic performance of little consequence. But if, on the other hand, the music is 'sweet' (V.v.42) but sad, ethereal and unlocalized, its 'disordered string' (V.v.46) might sound a note of immediate concord with Richard's poetry. This kind of music creates no broader perspective; the theatre creates music for Richard's benefit and joins him in insisting that there is nothing in the world outside his prison cell.

50–66 This latter kind of music seems to me to be what is demanded by the text, though other kinds of music are not incompatible with the interpretation I am about to develop of the final movement of the speech. Richard seems, with his 'Now, sir', at the beginning of line 55, to realize that in spite of his desire for nothingness and invisibility, the theatre is his most potent ally in creating an imaginative version of himself that the audience has almost no choice but to prefer over Bolingbroke. 'Now, sir' demands that the actor playing Richard approach the edge of the stage and explain his point of view to a particular spectator; 'Now, sir' is an exciting moment of intimacy between actor and spectator that insists upon the compelling idea that the theatre is all around us no matter where we are, that we are of the same substance as Richard because we share his nothingness. 'Now, sir' is not the kind of thing Bolingbroke, proficient performer though he may be, could ever say. The nature and method of Bolingbroke's theatricality is to keep artifice and reality carefully separated. With 'Now, sir', Richard convinces at least one of us that he is well beyond such a crude understanding of theatrical power.

67–97 The Groom of the stable who enters at line 67 is the theatre's last gift to Richard. He enters with the same feeling of eerie and arbitrary significance as the music a couple dozen lines earlier. Who let the Groom into the prison? Even Richard is somewhat surprised at lines 69–71 that he would have been let in or able to find the place. What is the Groom's purpose for visiting? Why would his current master have given him 'leave / To look upon my sometime master's face' (V.v.74–5)? What does he mean when, exiting at line 97, he says 'What my tongue does not, that my heart shall say?' The Groom's thoughts and motivations as an individual, as a theatrical 'person', must almost inevitably remain mysterious, but his theatrical effect, as part of the reflective structure the play builds around Richard, is fairly clear. Immediately following the moment in Richard's soliloquy ('Now, sir') where the former king intimately acknowledges the presence of an audience on whom he depends for sympathy and power, the Groom's entrance and his protestations of love for his former master give the lie to the posture of distance and snobbery that Richard cultivated in I.iv. Describing Bolingbroke's usurpation of Richard's horse and the fickle beast's ignorant pride at having so fine a rider on its back, the Groom makes us feel that loyal service to Richard, however difficult it might be, is an honourable thing, and that shifting allegiance to Bolingbroke can only be done unthinkingly. In the next scene, we will see an inverted echo of the Groom in the character of Exton, who gives us the first clear indication of what it means to serve such a master as Bolingbroke.

98 to the end   It is just possible that an audience, aware of the fact that Richard must die soon, thinks that the Groom is an agent of Bolingbroke and Exton, and that our experience of their conversation is one of suspense as we wonder whether it will suddenly turn violent. Richard may share this fear, and his worry may carry over to the entrance of the Keeper, whom he immediately commands to taste the food he's brought in. Is this Richard's killer? When the keeper mentions 'Sir Pierce of Exton' (V.v.100) the audience may feel a jolt of recognition: now the end is upon Richard. (An audience, or a spectator, unfamiliar, or not deeply familiar, with Holinshed may not feel the jolt of recognition, especially since Exton was not named in V.iv. Possibly the scene is meant to leave both Richard and audience in ongoing suspense about which character will be his murderer.) As Richard curses 'Henry of Lancaster, and thee', he probably overturns whatever dishes have been brought to him, and perhaps he turns his anger physically against the Keeper. While both Quarto and Folio texts print the stage direction calling for the entrance of the murderers after the Keeper's 'Help, help, help!' it might be possible to stage the scene so that the Keeper's cry is a response to (rather than a call for) the sudden entrance of Exton and his men. Like the Groom, the Keeper might be a lower-class ally to Richard rather than part of Bolingbroke's vast network of violent subordinates.

In what we might see as typically self-aggrandizing fashion, Richard's reaction to the entrance of Exton is virtually to allegorize it, seeing the assassination as an assault not simply by Bolingbroke, but by 'Death' itself. (The word is capitalized in both Quarto and Folio texts as well as in the Signet.) But while it is traditional to see this kind of self-aggrandizing theatricality as an example of how Richard is effete and disconnected from reality, it is important to note that he demonstrates a very real, physical power in his final moments. His lines at 106 and 108 indicate that he kills two of Exton's men before Exton is able to kill him. Exton is impressed: 'As full of valor as of royal blood!' (V.v.113). This line may also be a cue to the playing company that Richard's death is to be accompanied by a lot of stage blood, that we are meant to have an intense awareness of his physical being even as the last thing Richard imagines for himself is his soul mounting 'on high' (V.v.111). A further reminder of the physicality of death can come from the problem of getting Richard's body, and the bodies of the two men he killed, off the stage. A modern playing company can, of course, use a blackout or a curtain to allow the actors to get up and off the stage without breaking the illusion. But in Shakespeare's theatre Exton and any of his remaining helpers would have probably had to drag the 'dead' bodies of the actors off the stage. Our last image of the body of Richard in this kind of theatre – we only see the coffin that encloses it in V.vi – is one where it is an unwieldy, bloody mess, literally staining the land (see V.v.110) as Exton drags it off. This body is also, at last, indistinguishable from the 'beggars' who have brought about its end; it is now simply a pile of 'gross flesh' on its way to becoming earth.

Act V, scene vi

1–29   The last scene of the play is the first scene in which Bolingbroke can be said to have actual and complete control of the kingdom. Remarkably, this scene is characterized by an insistent sense of uncertainty: this is how Shakespeare dramatizes the realities of royal power.

Bolingbroke enters talking to York about the rebels' burning of Ciceter, and says he does not know whether or not the royalist forces have been victorious. Bolingbroke is in a position we have not seen him in since his arrival back in England in II.iii: he is not sure exactly what is going on and is dependent upon others for information; his control of the kingdom seems to hang in the balance. It is true that Bolingbroke very quickly gets good news about the Oxford rebellion, but the slightly off-balance way in which the scene begins importantly characterizes the beginning of his reign. The more predictable way for this scene to begin would have been for Bolingbroke to enter explaining to York, or hearing from Northumberland and Fitzwater, that the rebels had been suppressed. The Bolingbroke who was at the centre of events, controlling his own destiny, is gradually becoming the Bolingbroke of 1 *Henry IV* – the Bolingbroke who is relatively isolated from the conflicts broiling around him and who is overly dependent upon the Percies for aid and information.

The Bolingbroke of this scene might also be performed as becoming the myopically self-interested king of 1 *Henry IV*, whose ingratitude to his allies ultimately causes them to turn against him. His expressions of gratitude are no more substantive in this scene than they were in II.iii, before he could really promise anyone anything. 'We thank thee gentle Percy, for thy pains, / And to thy worth will add right worthy gains', he tells Northumberland at lines 11–12. The combination of the rhyme and the vagueness of 'right worthy gains' makes this seem like the perfunctory performance of gratitude. So too with his thanks to Fitzwater at lines 17–8 – a kind of boilerplate repetition of what he already said to Northumberland. Perhaps most significantly, Bolingbroke has no words of thanks for young Harry Percy, who brings in the Bishop of Carlisle. Perhaps the actor playing Hotspur reacts to this potential slight with silent, indignant surprise, giving the audience a sense of a relationship suddenly severed – and another one re-formed – as young Percy goes to stand by his father. The attitude projected by Harry Percy and his father Northumberland, who were so instrumental in setting Bolingbroke up, is crucial for preparing – or failing to prepare – the audience for what is to come in the next part of the historical narrative.

30 to the end   Bolingbroke's apparent ingratitude to Northumberland, Fitzwater, and Harry Percy is equivocal enough that an actor need not play it as such; it would be easy enough to play these moments as conventional but genuine gestures of thanks necessary to wrap up the historical plot fairly quickly. Such is not the case with Bolingbroke's ingratitude toward Exton. Here we see most clearly what King Henry IV is made of.

It may be that Bolingbroke does not expect the arrival of Exton and the coffin. He has not mentioned Richard's death to anyone on stage so far, and Exton's appearance in this public setting would seem to run counter to the secrecy Exton himself had earlier attributed to Bolingbroke's desire for the assassination. I imagine a two-levelled staging in this scene. Exton arrives and announces with great formality, as the coffin is placed centre-stage, that he has brought the body of 'The mightiest of thy greatest enemies, / Richard of Bordeaux' (V.vi.32–3). It is worth noting that Exton carefully avoids saying anything about having killed, or having been asked to kill, Richard. His arrival, however, is a surprise, registered visibly on the faces not only of Northumberland, Harry Percy, and Fitzwater, but also, for a tense but fleeting moment, of Bolingbroke himself. Bolingbroke recovers quickly, though, and escorts Exton downstage to talk quietly with him while the others look into the coffin, beholding the dead former king. With astonishing brutality, Bolingbroke transfers all of his guilt to Exton (at line 43 he equates him with the original murderer of kinsmen, Cain) and dismisses him with 'neither my good word, nor princely favor' (V.vi.42). Exton's silence as he exits might be furious and ominous – a clear indication that he, as well as the Percies, might be back to haunt the new king; or it might be utterly defeated – a concession to Bolingbroke's absolute authority and to the irrevocable damage Richard's murder has done. After Exton is gone – and perhaps even as he is in the very act of leaving – Bolingbroke returns to centre-stage and begins to perform. 'Lords', he says, 'I protest my soul is full of woe' (V.vi.45), and he plans a perfectly appointed gesture – dressed in black, journeying to the Holy Land – to counteract the transgression of his rebellion. The 'Lords' he addresses are, of course, Northumberland, Harry Percy, and Fitzwater, but his focus is also directed outward, at the audience. In spite of what we know about his conversation with Exton, Bolingbroke performs his pity for us, conscripts us into his theatrical monarchy, has no doubt that we will applaud after he has finished speaking. He is the embodiment of an efficiently performative power that we knew was lacking, and that we often desired, in Richard; he is the father of Henry V and the forerunner of a golden age for England; we are his subjects.

3 The Play's Sources and Cultural Context

English history in the Elizabethan repertory theatre

By the time Shakespeare was writing *Richard II*, the English history play was an established and popular genre on the London stage. Shakespeare, in the earlier part of his theatrical career, had done much to make this a reality. Among the first plays Shakespeare wrote upon arriving in London were the three *Henry VI* plays: these sprawling plays combine the epic violence of dramatic texts like Marlowe's 1 and 2 *Tamburlaine* with historical narratives in the tradition of those popularized in the late 1580s by the Queen's Men (*The Famous Victories of Henry V, The True Tragedy of Richard III, The Troublesome Reign of King John*). Contemporary with the *Henry VI* plays were George Peele's *Edward I* (*c.* 1591), Robert Greene's *The Scottish History of James IV* (*c.* 1591), Marlowe's *Edward II* (*c.* 1592), the anonymous *Jack Straw* (*c.* 1591), and possibly the anonymous *Thomas of Woodstock* (*c.* 1591–5). Almost all of these plays have in common a highly episodic, sometimes even chaotic style, where the monarch is not necessarily the central focus: 'elevated' political intrigue and 'low' episodes involving commoners are placed side by side so that neither one seems to have priority over the other. The plays are often geographically ambitious, shuttling spectators rapidly across England, or between England and the Continent, so that the Court is never quite able to come into focus as a *centre* of power.

Starting with *Richard III*, Shakespeare began to write a somewhat different kind of history play, one whose narrative is focused more tightly around a single protagonist and whose protagonist explicitly and consistently establishes himself as the centre of the narrative by means of self-consciously theatrical engagement with the audience. This new kind of history play adapts historical narrative to the formal conventions of theatrical tragedy and works to make the central historical figure a kind of tragic hero, a great man destroyed by forces beyond his control which he himself unleashes. The simultaneously introspective and histrionic character of Richard II is a type that Shakespeare had already experimented with in *Titus Andronicus* (c. 1592), and that he would perfect in *Hamlet* (c. 1600). In this respect it is significant that, through its 1615 printing, the title page of all the play's quartos called the play the *Tragedy* of Richard II. Only in the Folio, where perhaps the formal imperatives of a 'collected works' edition caused the compilers to define the play more narrowly than it might originally have been, is the play classified as a one of the 'Histories', and titled, like *Richard III*, as a play about the *Life and Death* of its monarch.

The histrionic, tragic monarch is, of course, not a Shakespearean invention. We see such a character in Marlowe's Edward II or *True Tragedy*'s Richard III. But beginning with *Richard III* and continuing through *Henry V*, Shakespeare undertakes a sustained and searching exploration of the relationship between the theatre and competing notions of political power. In the Shakespearean version of history that held the stage in 1593–9, the star actor, using language and metaphors particular to his craft in order to express the existential quandaries particular to the person of a king, is given extraordinary power to shape popular understanding of monarchical identity. In Shakespeare's staging of English history, the language of the theatre comes to seem an inevitable and essential means by which to understand political and historical process. This self-authorizing self-consciousness is undoubtedly a large part of why Shakespeare's history plays continue to maintain such a hold upon the popular imagination. Rather than rehearsing the conventional distinction between 'performance' and 'reality', these plays convince us that reality lies *within* performance.

History plays continued to be quite popular until the early seventeenth century, by which time the genre seems to have exhausted itself: over the course of 20 years or so, starting in the 1580s, the commercial theatre had managed to stage a play dealing with the reign or part of the reign of every English monarch from Henry II to Elizabeth I. The plays contemporaneous with Shakespeare's second phase of history writing, from *Richard III* through *Henry V*, underwent a change of form as well. The history plays of Shakespeare's contemporaries in the middle and later 1590s are newly, explicitly focused on theatricality. However, the formal consequence of this new focus is not a tighter relationship between protagonist and narrative. Rather, it is a morphing of historical narrative into disguise comedy. Henry Chettel and Anthony Munday's *Robert Earl of Huntingdon* plays (1598), the anonymous *Look About You* (1599), and the collaborative 1 *Sir John Oldcastle* (1599) and *The Blind Beggar of Bednal Green* (1600) all represent English history as a combination of folk legend and contemporary popular comedy, where royal power is constantly challenged and undercut by crafty commoners and the mechanics of disguise-centred intrigue result, ultimately, in the restoration of social and civic harmony. These plays are generally compared unfavourably to Shakespeare's histories. Yet, they should not be understood as competing with Shakespeare on his own terms (though there was certainly an element of commercial competition). Instead, they should been seen as presenting an alternative ethos of theatrical politics. A simple way of describing this ethos would be to say that, for the authors of these plays, merging the genres of history play and disguise comedy becomes a way of expressing the idea that political power *need not* be understood in terms of theatrical performance. For these authors, there is a moment when costumes can come off, acting can stop, and 'truth' can be revealed. It is a more hopeful (if perhaps less realistic) vision of the theatre and of history than Shakespeare tends to offer.

The foregoing observations about trends in the structure of history plays in the later 1590s are simplified and inevitably based on incomplete information. The disguise-comedy model outlined above as an alternative to Shakespeare's star-centred model is mainly characteristic of extant plays from a single playing company, the Admiral's Men. There are many lost Admiral's plays (*Henry I*, for example, in 1597, or *Robert II, King of Scots* in 1599) that may or may not have fallen into the category I have created. Other playwrights were experimenting with other forms: Heywood's *Edward IV* plays (written for Derby's men in 1599) hearken back to the dramaturgy of history plays of the early 1590s; the anonymous *Edward III* (1595, performed by an unknown company) and *Thomas Lord Cromwell* (1602, probably performed by Chamberlain's Men) are more similar to what we have come to think of as the Shakespearean history play. And it is also important to note that even as Shakespeare began, in the mid 1590s, to write a different kind of history play, he almost always made use of the episodic structure characteristic of the earliest history plays. This is structure that deliberately complicated the monarch as a central figure and which was a characteristic of the earliest history plays. There is one exception to this generalization about Shakespeare's history play – one play that seems particularly to subvert the conventions of historical dramaturgy as they had developed and would continue to develop; one play that is particularly emphatic in its location of historical meaning in the performance of the King and thus the person of the actor. That play is *Richard II*.

The reign of Richard II as a political allegory

In the same way that early modern tragedies like *Othello* or *The Duchess of Malfi* reflected popular conceptions of and fears about marriage and female sexuality, early modern history plays reflected popular conceptions of and fears about foreign policy and domestic political stability. Shakespeare's *Henry V* is not only an expression of nostalgia for a glorious moment in English political and military history; it is also, in its representation of a young monarch at the height of his powers, an instance of theatrical wish fulfilment for a populace living in the reign of an aging and ailing Queen, whose doubtful succession left the nation vulnerable to foreign predators. The anonymous *Look About You* is not only a fanciful imagining of political in-fighting in terms of petty domestic squabbles; it is also, in its situating an archetypal English royal family (that of Henry II) in a disguise-comedy plot, an optimistic recasting of contemporary anxieties about Elizabeth's lack of an heir. Because they are always to some degree built upon a teleological view of English history – all ages working toward the age of Elizabeth – English history plays of the sixteenth century, no matter what period they represent, always contain the potential to be understood as at least partial allegories for late sixteenth-century politics.

More so than other English monarchs, Richard II served a particularly explicit allegorical function for early modern English playwrights. Early modern playwrights were always fairly careless and/or expedient in their handling of source material. They were always willing to manipulate details and chronology in the historical record for the sake of a particular theatrical effect. This seems to have been even more emphatically the case with the reign of Richard II. Thus the anonymous *Jack Straw* (published in 1593), which represents the 1381 uprising known as the Peasants' Rebellion – one of the first major challenges faced by the young king Richard – does not even give its King character a name, and presents its action as a series of didactic and semi-allegorical tableaux where the King and his advisors discuss how important it is for a King to treat his loyal subjects justly. *Thomas of Woodstock*, probably written and performed a year or two before Shakespeare's play (though there is some debate about this) deals with events from the middle of Richard's reign, when Richard faced and suppressed rebellion from a powerful Court faction led by his uncle Woodstock. Although all sources confirm Holinshed's description of Woodstock as 'hastie, wilfull, and given more to war than peece', the anonymous author of *Woodstock* represents him as a good-natured, plain-spoken man who suffers unjustly at the hands of a wanton and rapacious king. As with *Jack Straw*, the style of *Woodstock* is explicitly moralistic and semi-allegorical, much given to the expression of generalized indictments of unjust governance rather than representation of problems particular to Richard II's reign. While Shakespeare's play, with its elaborate representations of medieval pageantry (I.i and I.iii) and its naturalistic representation of the mechanics of Bolingbroke's rebellion, conveys a greater sense of temporal specificity than *Jack Straw* or *Woodstock*, it is equally wanton in its handling of source material, imagining (especially in the Garden scene or the Prison scene) Richard and his Queen as archetypal representations of problems of royal power rather than as historical personages responding to particular historical circumstances. This is almost the exact opposite of Shakespeare's method in the *Henry VI* plays.

The peculiar abstractness of plays about Richard II in the early modern period makes their potential allegorical elements all the more vivid. The didactic and/or archetypal elements can make the plays seem as though they are to be construed as cautionary tales to monarchs in general: deposition and murder are the inevitable consequences that await leaders who do not heed, or who misperceive the loyalty of, their powerful allies. This was the message the Earl of Essex and his supporters seem to have intended to convey when they ordered a production of the play on the eve of their rebellion. But of course the failure of the play to provoke popular support for the rebellion suggests rather powerfully the way in which the message of *Richard II* as a cautionary tale is a profoundly mixed one. However uncertain an audience in 1595–6 might have felt about the domestic and foreign consequences of their heirless Queen's imminent death, they would certainly have had the historiographic materials at their disposal to understand that the heirless monarch represented on the stage before them was emphatically *different from* Queen Elizabeth; to think, for example, of his death as a necessary destruction of weakness in order to pave the way for the medieval antecedent to Elizabeth's glory, Henry V. The fact that Richard was popularly represented as an effeminate, or even partially feminine King (see, especially, V.v.5–11) might be seen, on one hand, as a means by which he can be understood as an allegory for Elizabeth. On the other hand, it might be seen as a means by which the two can be differentiated: Richard, finally and destructively, imagines himself as containing something essentially feminine; Elizabeth, famously and triumphantly while addressing her army at Tilbury as it prepared to confront the Spanish Armada, imagined herself as containing something essentially masculine: 'I know I have but the body of a weak and feeble woman; but I have the heart and stomach of a king, and of a king of England, too.'

So it is clear that the reign of Richard II resonated particularly strongly in the imagination of those subjects of Elizabeth who were interested in thinking of her history in terms of prior history, but I do not think it is clear exactly what the resonances were, or how they came about. It may have been a simple matter of coincidence and expediency: the question of succession was a particularly urgent one in the latter years of Elizabeth's reign; no earlier English society faced with similarly urgent questions (the England under Edward III, for example) had had the benefit of an elaborate professional entertainment industry to dramatize its anxieties in the moment and (through printed texts) for posterity; Richard's childlessness and the dramatic simplicity of the narrative of his deposition might have made his reign particularly attractive to a variety of kinds of early modern playwright. And even as *Richard II*'s potential allegorical relationship with late sixteenth-century politics, and the possibility of censorship in the deposition scene, suggest that it was at least potentially incendiary during the reign of Elizabeth, we must also note that its history during the reign of James does not conform to what we might expect. In the early years of his reign James was no less embattled than Elizabeth was in the latter years of hers: the Gunpowder Plot of November 1605, when Catholic conspirators were foiled in an attempt to blow up the Houses of Parliament, is only the most vivid example of the thin ice on which the new King walked. Moreover, whether or not James was more politically embattled than Elizabeth, he was a much more active censor of drama than she was; for example, he ordered Jonson, Marston, and Chapman jailed for inappropriate satire in *Eastward Ho*. And yet *Richard II*'s longer deposition scene, where a King gives the crown to his usurper, appeared for the first time in 1608, five years after James ascended to the throne.

The sources of *Richard II*

In *Richard II*, Shakespeare deals with the very end of Richard's reign from April 1398 to February 1400. The principal source from which Shakespeare drew his information about the events of these 22 months is Raphael Holinshed's *Chronicles of England, Scotland, and Ireland* (1587). There are also a number of sources that can be seen to have influenced Shakespeare's play more or less directly. From Edward Hall's *Union of the Two Noble and Illustre Families of Lancastre and York*, he may have got the idea to begin the play with the quarrel between Mowbray and Bolingbroke. While there are few verbal correspondences between *Richard II* and the *Union*, Shakespeare made use of Hall in the *Henry VI* plays, and so would presumably have been familiar with that source's treatment of Richard II. As noted in Chapter 1, Shakespeare seems to have been indebted to Samuel Daniel's poem about the English civil wars for his unhistorical but highly poetic representation of the relationship between Richard and his Queen. It is possible that Shakespeare was also familiar with the medieval French chronicler Froissart, whose *Chronicle* was translated into English in 1523 and used extensively by Holinshed, and whose portraits of Gaunt and of Richard's marriage to his French Queen resemble Shakespeare's in some respects. The anonymous play *Woodstock*, if it was written before *Richard II*, would almost certainly have been a play Shakespeare was familiar with; this is true of *Jack Straw* as well, which definitely preceded *Richard II*. While each of these plays – and *Woodstock* in particular – might be seen to have echoes in Shakespeare's (the Woodstock of the earlier play seems to be who Gaunt has in mind at II.i.126–31), neither can properly be considered a 'source' text. Unlike Holinshed's *Chronicles*, written two decades earlier (the first edition was published in 1577) and for an entirely different purpose, *Woodstock* and *Jack Straw* were written for the same theatrical world of which Shakespeare was a part, and can therefore more accurately be understood as distinct but related commercially driven popular reimaginings of the figure of Richard.

Source study provides many tempting and potentially productive opportunities for interpretation in the study of Shakespeare in performance, but it is worth scrutinizing these opportunities fairly carefully rather than simply accepting their value. The most common interpretive move in the study of sources and performance is to look at the source text – Holinshed's description of Woodstock, for example – then to look at a moment when we might expect correspondence in the play text – what Gaunt says about Woodstock in *Richard II* II.i – and finally to use the difference between the two moments, often filtered through performance, as a basis for interpretation: if Gaunt means, or the Gaunt actor speaks, the lines earnestly, we can understand Shakespeare's project as involving, in part, a deliberate revision of documentary history; if Gaunt intends, or the Gaunt actor speaks the lines in such a way as, to indicate that he is merely giving voice to the official view of Woodstock, then we can understand Shakespeare's project as involving, in part, a self-conscious examination of the uses to which history is put by those who are in the process of making it. As useful as such an exercise might be to an actor or a director or a teacher, it has the disadvantage of perpetually reinscribing the source *text* as the point from which *theatrical* meanings originate, and with respect to which they are measured. One of my main goals in this section has been to give a sense of the degree to which Shakespeare's *Richard II* is for the most part only tangentially related to what are conventionally understood as its 'historical context' and its 'historical sources'. I use the figure of the *tangent* quite literally here: from any number of contextual perspectives, *Richard II* can be seen as a textual and theatrical event that intersects briefly with a single, precise point on the edge of a sphere called *history* or *politics* or *source-text* before continuing on its own course.

It is with this analogy in mind that I present the following eclectic gathering of excerpts from some of *Richard II*'s 'sources' and from some of the theatrical texts roughly contemporaneous with it. A reader interested in seeing 'how Shakespeare deviated from his source' need only read Holinshed's description of Richard's reign to see how little Shakespeare was 'inspired' by history and how interested he was to imagine a Richard almost wholly his own. I have tried with the selection of materials presented below to present a vivid if slightly chaotic mosaic of narrative, poetic, and theatrical ideas about Richard II in circulation in the mid 1590s; my idea of the importance of this mosaic is not so much, or not only, that it would have influenced Shakespeare's thinking about his subject in a systematic or thoroughgoing way, but that it might have influenced the thinking of his *audience* in a sporadic, impressionistic way.

* * *

All but one of the following excerpts has been transcribed from original documents. My modernized transcription of the excerpt from *Woodstock*, whose only authoritative early text is a manuscript, was made from the 1929 Malone Society transcription of that manuscript. In all the excerpts I have modernized the spelling, but left the punctuation as near as possible to the original.

From *Holinshed's Chronicles* (1587)

Richard's coronation

The king, in riding through the city towards Westminster, on the 15 day of July being Wednesday, was accompanied with such a train of the nobility and others, as in such case was requisite ... The noise of trumpets and other instruments was marvelous, so that this seemed a day of joy and mirth, a day that had been long looked for, because it was hoped, that now the quiet orders and good laws of the land, which through the slothfulness of the aged king deceased, and covetousness of those that ruled about him, had been long banished, should now be renewed and brought again in use. The city was adorned in all sorts most richly. The water conduits ran with wine for the space of three hours together. In the upper end of Cheape, was a certain castle made with four towers, out of which castle, on two sides of it, there ran forth wine abundantly. In the towers were placed four beautiful virgins, of stature and age like to the king, appareled in white vestures, in every tower one, the which blew in the kings face, at his approaching near to them, leaves of gold, and as he approached also, they threw on him and his horse florins of gold counterfeit....

That done, there was sermon preached by a bishop touching the duty of a king, how he ought to behave himself towards the people, and how the people ought to be obedient unto him. The sermon being ended, the king received his oath before the archbishop and nobles: which done, the archbishop having the lord Henry Percy lord marshal going before him, turned him to every quarter of the church, declaring to the people the king's oath, and demanding of them, if they would submit themselves unto such a prince & governor, and obey his commandments: and when the people with a loud voice had answered that they would obey him, the archbishop using certain prayers, blessed the king; which ended, the archbishop came unto him, and tearing his garments from the highest part to the lowest, stripped him to his shirt. Then was brought by earls, a certain coverture of cloth of gold, under the which he remained, whilest he was anointed....

After this, the archbishop did put upon him an uppermost vesture, called a pall, saying, Accipe pallium, &c. In the mean time, whilest the archbishop blessed the king's crown, he to whose office it appertained, did put spurs on his heels. After the crown was blessed, the archbishop set it on his head, saying, Coronet te Deus, &c....

In the mean time, sir John Dimmocke that claimed to be the king's champion, had been at the king's armory and stable, where he had chosen according to his tenure, the best armour save one, and the best steed save one...the said sir John Dimmocke having armed himself, and being mounted on horseback, came to the abbey gates, with two riding before him, the one carrying his spear, and the other his shield, staying there till mass should be ended. But the lord Henry Percy lord marshal, appointed to make way before the king with the duke of Lancaster lord Steward, the lord Thomas of Woodstoke lord constable, and the lord marshal's brother sir Thomas Percy, being all mounted on great horses, came to the knight, and told him, that he ought not to come at that time, but when the king was at dinner, and therefore it should be good for him to unarm himself for a while, and take his ease and rest, till the appointed time were come.

The knight did as the lord marshal willed him, and so after his departure, the king having those lords riding afore him, was borne on knights shoulders unto his palace, and so had to his chamber, where he rested a while, being somewhat faint with travel, and took a small refection.

Richard's death

And immediately after, king Henry, to rid himself of any such like danger to be attempted against him thereafter, caused king Richard to die of a violent death, that no man should afterward faine himself to represent his person, though some have said, he was not privy to that wicked offense. The common fame is, that he was every day served at the table with costly meat, like a king, to the intent that no creature should suspect any thing done contrary to the order taken in the parliament; and when the meat was set before him, he was forbidden once to touch it; yea, he was not permitted so much as to smell to it, and so he died of forced famine.

But Thomas Walsingham is so far from imputing his death to compulsory famine, that he referreth it altogether to voluntary pining of himself. For when he heard that the complots and attempts of such his favourers, as sought his restitution, and their own advancement, annihilated; and the chief agents shamefully executed; he took such a conceit at these misfortunes … that willfully he starved himself, and so died in Pomfret castle on S. Valentine's day: a happy day to him, for it was the beginning of his ease, and the ending of his pain: so that death was to him dainty and sweet ….

One writer, which seemeth to have great knowledge of king Richard's doings, saith, that king Henry, sitting on a day at his table, sore sighing, said, 'Have I no faithful friend which will deliver me of him, whose life will be my death, and whose death will be the preservation of my life?' This saying was much noted of them which were present, and especially of one called sir Piers of Exton. This knight incontinently departed from the court, with eight strong persons in his company, and came to Pomfret, commanding the esquire that was accustomed to sew and take the assay before king Richard, to do so no more, saying: 'Let him eat now, for he shall not long eat.' King Richard sat down to dinner, and was served without courtesy or assay, whereupon much marveling at the sudden change, he demanded of the esquire why he did not his duty; 'Sir (said he) I am otherwise commanded by sir Piers of Exton, which is newly come from K. Henry.' When king Richard heard that word, he took the carving knife in his hand, and strake the esquire on the head, saying 'The devil take Henry of Lancaster and thee together.' And with that word, sir Piers entered the chamber, well armed, with eight tall men likewise armed, every of them having a bill in his hand.

King Richard perceiving this, put the table from him, and stepping to the foremost man, wrung the bill out of his hands, and so valiantly defended himself, that he slew four of those that thus came to assail him. Sir Piers being half dismayed herewith, leapt into the chair where king Richard was wont to sit, while the other four persons fought with him, and chased him about the chamber. And in conclusion, as king Richard traversed his ground, from one side of the chamber to an other, and coming by the chair, where sir Piers stood, he was felled with a stroke of a poleax which sir Piers gave him upon the head, and therewith rid him out of life, without giving him respite once to call to God for mercy of his past offences.

From 'Howe kyng Richarde the seconde was for his evyll governaunce deposed from his seat, and miserably murdred in prison', in A *Myrroure for Magistrates* (1559)

I am a King that ruled all by lust,
That forced not of vertue, right, or law,
But alway put false Flatterers most in trust,
Ensuing such as could my vices claw:
By faithful counsel passing not a straw.
What pleasure prick'd, that thought I to be just.
I set my minde, to feede, to spoile, to joust,
Three meales a day could scarce content my maw,
And all to augment my lecherous mind that must
To Venus pleasures alway be in awe.
For maintenance wherof, my realm I polled
Through Subsidies, sore fines, loans, many I press'd,

Blank charters, oaths, & shifts not known of old,
For which my Subjects did me sore detest.
I also made away the towne of Brest.
My fault wherein because mine uncle told
(For Prince's vices may not be controlled)
I found the means his bowels to unbreast.
The Peers and Lords that did his cause uphold,
With death, exile, or grievous sins oppressed.
Neither lack'd I aid in any wicked deed,
For gaping Gulls whom I promoted had
Would further all in hope of higher meed.
A king can never imagine ought so bad
But most about him will perfume it glad
For sickness seldom doth so swiftly breed
As vicious humors grow the grief to feed.
Thus kings' estates of all be worst bestead,
Abused in wealth, abandoned at need,
And nearest harm when they be least adrad.
        My life and death the truth of this can try:
For while I fought in Ireland with my foes,
Mine uncle Edmund whom I left to guide
My realm at home, right traitorously arose
To help the Percies plying my depose,
And called from France Earl Bolenbroke, whom I
Condemned ten years in exile to lye:
Who cruelly did put to death all those
That in mine aid durst look but once awry,
Whose number was but slender I suppose.

From Anon., *Thomas of Woodstock* (c. 1591–5) Richard, reaching the age of 21, takes full control of his kingdom

Enter King Richard, Bagot, Bushy, Green, & Scroop & others
    Green. Yonder's your uncle, my lord.
    King. Aye, with our plain protector.
Full of complaints sweet Green, I'll wage my crown.
    Bagot. Give them fair words & smooth a while
The toils are pitch'd & you may catch them quickly.
    King. Why how now uncle, what disrob'd again
Of all your golden rich habiliments?

Woodstock. Be you then pleased good coz to hear me speak
And view they subjects sad petitions.
See here king Richard. Whilst thou livest at ease,
Lulling thy self in nice security,
Thy wronged kingdom's in a mutiny.
From every province are the people come
With open mouths exclaiming on the wrongs
Thou & these upstarts have imposed on them.
Shame is deciphered on thy palace gate,
Confusion hangeth o'er thy wretched head,
Mischief is coming & in storms must fall—
Th' oppression of the poor, to heaven doth call.

    King. Well well good uncle these your bitter taunts
Against my friends & me will one day cease.
But what's the reason you have sent for us?

    Lancaster. To have your grace confirm this parliament
And set your hand to certain articles
Most needful for your state & kingdom's quiet.

    King. Where are those articles?

    Arundel. The states & burgesses o' th' parliament
Attend with duty to deliver them.

    York. Please you ascend your throne, we'll call them in.

    King. We'll ask a question first, & then we'll see them
For trust me reverent uncles we have sworn
We will not sit upon our royal throne
Until this question be resolv'd at full.
Reach me that paper Bushy; hear me princes:
We had a strange petition here deliver'd us,
A poor man's son, his father being deceas'd,
Gave him in charge unto a rich man's hands
To keep him & the little land he had
Till he attained to 21 years.
The poor revenue amounts but to 3 crowns
And yet th' insatiate churl denies his right
And bars him of his fair Inheritance.
Tell me, I pray, will not our English laws
Enforce this rich man to resign his due?

    Woodstock. There is no let to bar it, gracious sovereign.
Afore my god, sweet prince, it joys my soul
To see your grace in person thus to judge his cause.

    York. Such deeds as this will make King Richard shine
Above his famous predecessor kings

If thus he labor to establish right.

    King. The poor man then had wrong, you all confess?

    Woodstock. And shall have right, my liege, to quit his wrong.
Then Woodstock give us right, for we are wrong'd.
Thou art the rich, & we the poor man's son.
The realms of England, France, & Ireland
Are those 3 crowns thou yearly keep'st from us.
Is't not a wrong, when every mean man's son
May take his birthright at the time expired
And we, the principal, being now attain'd
Almost to 22 years of age,
Cannot be suffer'd to enjoy our own,
Nor peaceably possess our father's right?

    Woodstock. Was this the trick, sweet prince? Alack the day!
You need not thus have doubled with your friends.
The right I hold, even with my heart I render
And wish your grace had claimed it long ago.
Th'adst rid mine age of mickel care & woe
And yet I think I have not wrong'd your birthright,
For if the time were search'd I guess your grace
Is not so full of years til April next.
But be it as it will: lo, here King Richard,
I thus yield up my sad protectorship. *Gives the Mace up*
A heavy burden has thou ta'en from me.
Long mayest thou live in peace & keep thine own,
That truth & justice may attend thy throne.

    King. Then in the name of heaven we thus ascend it
And here we claim our fair inheritance
Of fruitful England, France, & Ireland,
Superior lord of Scotland, & the rights
Belonging to our great dominions.
Here, uncles, take the crown from Richard's hand
And once more place it on our kingly head.
This day we will be new enthronized.

From Anon., *The Life and Death of Jacke Straw* (c. 1591)

The young Richard II negotiates with the leaders of the peasants' rebellion

    Lord Mayor. It shall become your Grace most Gracious Lord,
To bear the mind in this afflicted time,

As other kings and Lords hath done before,
Armed with sufferance and magnanimity,
The one to make you resolute for chance,
The other forward in your resolution:
The greatest wrong this rout hath done your grace,
Amongst a many wicked parts,
Is in frighting your worthy Lady Mother,
Making foul slaughter of your noble men,
Burning up books and matters of records,
Defacing houses of hostility,
Saint John's in Smithfield, the Savoy and such like,
And beating down like wolves the better sort,
The greatest wrong in my opinion is,
That in honor doth your person touch:
I mean they call your Majesty to parley,
And overbear you with a multitude,
As if you were a vassal not a king.
O wretched minds of vild and barbarous men,
For whom the heavens have secret wreak in store:
But my Lord with reverence and with pardon too,
Why comes your Grace into Smithfield near the crew,
Unarm'd and guarded with so small a train?

    King. If clemency may win their raging minds,
To civil order, I'll approve it first
They shall perceive me come in quiet wise,
Accompanied with the Lord Mayor here alone,
Besides our Guard that attend on us.

    Lord Mayor. May it please your Grace that I shall raise the streets
To guard your Majesty through Smithfield as you walk?

    King. No Lord mayor, 't'will make them more outrageous,
And be a mean to shed a world of blood:
I more account the blood of Englishmen than so.
But this is the place I have appointed them,
To hear them speak and have adventured,
To come among this foul unruly crew:
And lo my Lords, see where the people comes.

Enter Jack Straw, Wat Tyler, Tom Miller, Parson Ball, and Hob Carter

    Jack Straw. My masters this is the king, come away,
This he that would speak withal.

    King. Newton, desire that one may speak for all,
To tell the sum of their demand at full.

    Newton. My masters you that are the special men,

His Majesty requires you and by me,
That one may speak and tell him your demand,
And gently here he lets you know by me,
He is resolv'd to hear him all at large.

 King. Aye, my good friends, I pray you heartily
Tell us your minds as nimbly as you can:
And we will answer you so well to all,
As you that shall not mislike in anything.

 Jack Straw. We come to revenge your officer's ill demeanor,
And though we have killed him for his knavery,
Now we be gotten together, we will have wealth and liberty.
Cry all: Wealth and liberty!

 King. It is enough believe me if you will,
For as I am your true succeeding Prince,
I swear by all the honor of my crown,
You shall have liberty and pardon all,
As God hath given it and your lawful king.

 Wat Tyler. Ere we'll be pinch'd with poverty,
To beg our meat and vittles from the ground,
That are as worthy of good maintenance,
As any Gentleman your Grace doth keep,
We will be kings and Lords within ourselves.
And not abide the pride the pride of tyranny.

 King. I pray thee fellow what country man art thou?

 Wat Tyler. It skills not much I am an English man.

 Ball. Marry sir he is a Kentishman, and hath been my scholar ere now.

 Lord Mayor. Little good manners hat the villain learn'd
To use his Lord and king so barbarously.

 King. Well people ask you any more,
Thank to be free and have your liberty.
Cry all: Wealth and liberty!

 King. Then take my word I promise to you all,
And eke my general pardon now forthwith,
Under my seal and letters patents to perform the same,
Let every man betake him to his home,
And with what speed our clerks can make dispatch,
Your pardons and your letters patents,
Shall be forthwith sent down in every shire.

 Hob Carter. Marry I think your Grace, Hob Carter and the Essex
Men will home again, and we will take your word.

 King. We believe you all and thank you all,
And presently we will commandment give,
That all this business may be quickly ready. *Exeunt King and his Train.*

From Samuel Daniel, *The First Fowre Bookes of the Ciuile Warres between the Two Houses of Lancaster and Yorke* (1595)

A description of the problems of the king's reign

Too many kings breed factions in the court,
The head too weak, the members grown too great:
O this is that which kingdoms doth transport,
This plague the heavens do for injustice threat
When children rule, who ever in this sort
Confound the state their ancestors did get;
For the ambitious once inur'd to reign
Can never brook a private state again.

And kingdoms ever suffer this distress,
For one or many guide the infant king,
Which one or many, tasting this excess,
Of greatness and command; can never bring
Their thoughts again t'obey or to be less:
From hence these insolencies ever spring,
Contempt of others whom they seek to foil,
Then follow leagues, destruction, ruin, spoil.

Whether it were that they which had the charge
Suffered the king to take a youthful vein,
That they their private better might enlarge:
Or whether he himself would farther strain
(Thinking his years sufficient to discharge
The government) presumed to take the reign,
We will not say: but now his ear he lends
To youthful counsel, and his lusts attends.

And courts were never barren yet of those
Which could with subtle train and apt advice
Work on the Prince's weakness, and dispose
Of feeble frailty easiest to entice:
And such no doubt about this king arose,
Whose flattery (the dangerous nurse of vice)
Got hand upon his youth to pleasures bent
Which led by them did others discontent.

The King and Queen

Now Isabell the young afflicted Queen,
Whose years had never shew'd her but delights,

Nor lovely eyes before had ever seen
Other than smiling joys and joyful sights:
Born great, match'd great, liv'd great and ever been
Partaker of the world's best benefits,
Had plac'd herself, hearing her Lord should pass,
That way where she unseen in secret was.

    Sick of delay and longing to behold
Her long miss'd love in fearful jeopardies,
To whom although it had in sort been told
Of their proceeding, and of his surprise,
Yet thinking they would never be so bold
To lead their Lord to any shameful wife,
But rather would conduct him as their king,
As seeking but the state's reordering.

    And forth she looks and notes the foremost train,
And grieves to view some there she wish'd not there,
Seeing the chief not come, stays, looks again,
And yet she sees not him that should appear:
Then back she stands, and then desires was fain
Again to look to see if he were near,
At length a glittering troop far off she spies,
Perceives the throng and hears the shouts & cries.

*　*　*

    Then forth she goes a close concealed way,
As grieving to be seen not as she was;
Labors t'attain his presence all she may,
Which with most hard ado was brought to pass:
For that night understanding where he lay
With earnest treating she procured her pass
To come to him. Rigor could not deny
Those tears, so poor a suit, or put her by.

    Entering the chamber where he was alone
As one whose former fortune was his shame,
Loathing th' upbraiding eye of any one
That knew him once and knows him not the same:
When having given express command that none
Should press to him, yet hearing some that came,
Turns angrily about his grieved eyes,
When lo his sweet afflicted Queen he spies.

    Straight clears his brow & with a borrowed smile

'What my dear Queen, O welcome dear,' he says,
And striving his own passion to beguile
And hide the sorrow which his eye betrays,
Could speak no more but wrings her hands
And then, 'Sweet lady,' and again he stays:
Th'excess of joy and sorrow both affords
Affliction none, or but poor niggard words.

　　　She that had come with a resolved heart
And a mouth full stor'd, with words well chose,
Thinking 'This comfort will I first impart
Unto my lord, and thus my speech dispose:
Then thus I'll say, thus look, and with this art
Hide mine own sorrow to relieve his woes,'
When being come all this prov'd naught but wind,
Tears, looks, and sighs do only tell her mind.

　　　Thus both stood silent and confused so,
Their eyes relating how their hearts did mourn,
Both big with sorrow, and both great with woe
In labor with what was not to be borne:
This mighty burden wherewithal they go
Dies undelivered, perishes unborn;
Sorrow makes silence her best orator
Where words may make it less not shew it more.

4 Critical Assessments

From Johnson to Yeats: the making of the Poet-King

Samuel Johnson did not like Shakespeare's *Richard II*, and he was lukewarm about his Richard II. 'The play is one of those which Shakespeare has apparently revised', he wrote in the concluding note to the play in his 1765 edition. But 'as success in works of invention is not always proportionate to labour, it is not finished at last with that happy force of his tragedies, nor can be said much to affect the passions or enlarge the understanding'. Of Richard, Johnson said (in a note on III.ii.93):

> It seems to be the design of the poet to raise Richard to esteem in his fall and consequently to interest the reader in his favour. He gives him only passive fortitude, the virtue of a confessor rather than of a king. In his prosperity we saw him imperious and oppressive but in his distress he is wise, patient and pious.

Algernon Swinburne, the cantankerously eloquent Victorian heir to Johnsonian criticism of Shakespeare, voiced similar ideas about the play as a whole, and was much less charitable on the question of Richard's character. Writing in 1909, Swinburne said that *Richard II* was 'unmistakably the author's first attempt at historic drama.... The grasp of character is uncertain; the exposition of event is inadequate. The reader or spectator unversed in the byways of history has to guess what has already happened.... He gets so little help or light from the poet that he can only guess at random....' (pp. 64–5). In his discussion of the character of Richard, whom he compares to Marlowe's Edward II, Swinburne echoes Johnson's feeling that in this play Shakespeare was working too hard: 'Marlowe did not spend a tithe [i.e. one tenth] of the words or a tithe of the pains on the presentation of a character neither more worthy of contempt nor less worth of compassion. And his Edward is at least as living and convincing, as tragic and pathetic a figure as Shakespeare's Richard' (p. 77). Much of the work of *Richard II* criticism from Johnson to the early twentieth century involved finding a critical vocabulary that would allow students of the play to see Shakespeare's characterization of Richard and his casual handling of historical detail as evidence of an artistic project that was commensurate with the play's frequently glorious poetic language.

Twentieth- and twenty-first-century admirers of *Richard II* have had, of course, a sympathetic critical tradition upon which to draw as well. Lewis Theobald, one of Shakespeare's eighteenth-century editors, wrote in his 1733 edition of the play that '*Shakespeare* had drawn K. *Richard*'s Character according to the best Accounts of History; that is, insolent, proud, and thoughtless in prosperity; dejected and desponding on the Appearance of Danger. But whatever Blemishes he had either in Temper or Conduct ... our Compassion for Him wipes out the Memory of such Spots.' A little less than a century later, in a lecture delivered in 1812, Samuel Taylor Coleridge echoed Theobald's sentiment about the historical veracity of Shakespeare's play, but did so on the basis of almost precisely opposite evidence: 'It is, perhaps the most purely historical of Shakespeare's dramas. There are not in it, as in the others, characters introduced merely for the purpose of giving a greater individuality and realness ... Shakespeare avails himself of every opportunity to effect the great object of the historic drama, that, namely, of familiarizing the people to the great names of their country ...' and of dramatizing historical events 'presented in their *results*'. For Theobald, Shakespeare represented historical truth by means of characterization, turning Richard into a figure worthy of tragic pity, even if he does not act as we might imagine a king should; for Coleridge he did so by means of action, conferring a mythical narrative structure upon familiar English history. Theobald and Coleridge are alike – and unlike Johnson and Swinburne – in their willingness to understand apparent faults in dramatic construction as purposeful and significant. The excesses of Richard's character or the gaps Shakespeare leaves in the historical record are ultimately intelligible as expressions of a particularly powerful (and Shakespearean) view of history. An early twentieth-century formulation of Theobald and Coleridge's thematic approach to theatrical excess, which at the same time acknowledged the reasonableness of objections such as Johnson and Swinburne's, was made by Agnes Mure Mackenzie in her 1927 *Playgoer's Handbook to the English Renaissance Drama*: in *Richard II*, the

> central point is the elaborate analysis of a character. It is not quite success-ful. Richard is wonderfully understood, but Shakespeare's concern is so absorbed by the hero in himself that he is as yet rather negligent of the action that should have revealed him.... [But] it is the first English play where the interest is primarily in the psychology – not the career – of an individual, so that although it is not among its writer's greatest work, it marks none the less a new epoch in the history of our drama'. (p. 244)

E. M. W. Tillyard expressed a similar point of view in 1934, arguing that Shakespeare's interest in historical narrative extended only so far as it served the function of 'putting Richard's character in differ-ent lights' (p. 244).

Many influential critical voices have been content to discard his-tory as a factor in the evaluation of *Richard II* and to lay emphasis entirely on characterization. Coleridge himself, in the same lecture quoted above, is much less interested in Shakespeare as a national poet, 'exciting a steady stream of patriotism' with his evocation of historical events, than in Shakespeare as a poet of the imagination.

> From the beginning to the end of the play [Richard] pours out all the peculiarities and powers of his mind...He scatters himself into a multitude of images, and in conclusion endeavors to shelter himself from that which is around him by a cloud of his own thoughts.... The whole is joined with the utmost richness and copiousness of thought, and were there an actor capable of representing Richard, the part would delight us more than any other of Shakespeare's masterpieces...I know of no character drawn by our great poet with such unequalled skill as that of Richard II. (Coleridge, 1960, pp. 146–7)

Coleridge's contemporary William Hazlitt found a similar remark-able variegation in the character of Richard. But Hazlitt's inter-pretation differs from Coleridge's in that he does not find Richard's character extraordinary and extravagant so much as universal: 'He is...human in his distresses; for to feel pain and sorrow, weakness, disappointment, remorse and anguish, is the lot of humanity, and we sympathize with him accordingly. The sufferings of the man make us forget that he ever was a king' (*Characters of Shakespeare's Plays*, p. 111).

Hazlitt's universalizing of Richard was echoed in the early twentieth century by W. B. Yeats, who argued that Shakespeare saw 'in Richard II the defeat that awaits all, whether they be Artist or Saint, who find themselves where men ask of them a rough energy and have nothing to give but contemplative virtue, whether lyrical phantasy, or sweetness of temper, or dreamy dignity, or love of God, or love of His creatures' (*Ideas of Good and Evil*, p. 159). It is hard not to feel that in this passage Yeats is writing as much about himself as about Shakespeare's Richard II – or himself mirrored in Shakespeare's Richard II – and this is important because Yeats was a poet. Yeats's interpretation of Richard as a poet is an example of the critical tradition's triumph over the self-consciously reasonable judgments of critics like Johnson or Swinburne. Shakespeare's apparent interest in language rather than action, in human emotion rather than historical events, came to be interpreted as the defining quality of the character of Richard, and Richard in turn could be seen as a kind of figure for the poet, for Shakespeare himself. In this respect it is significant that the meticulous and unsentimental historian and critic E. K. Chambers, in his introduction to his 1891 edition of the play, praised *Richard II* in terms that echoed Coleridge's claim that the character of Richard 'pours out all the peculiarities and powers of his mind'. The difference is that, for Chambers, it is Shakespeare who does the pouring: 'On the delineation of Richard all the resources of Shakespeare's genius have been poured: it is a work of art and of love' (p. xii).

Formal analysis: the language of *Richard II*

Twentieth- and twenty-first-century criticism of *Richard II* can be divided into a few broad groups, the largest of which is probably criticism that deals with formal aspects of the play's poetry, its densely ornate patterning, and its self-conscious concern with language. Richard D. Altick's essay, 'Symphonic Imagery in *Richard II*' (1947) can be seen to sound the keynote for this school of criticism, as he set out to account for the 'impression of harmony, of oneness, which we receive when we read the play or listen to its lines spoken on the stage' (p. 339). For Altick, the secret lay in the way 'certain multifold meanings are played upon throughout the five acts, recurring time after time like leitmotivs in music' (p. 339). Where some Victorian critics, such as Swinburne and Walter Pater, had seen much of *Richard II*'s poetry as highly ornamental, enlivening even the frequently trite sentiments of Richard with the 'gay, fresh, variegated flowers of speech' (Pater, p. 512), Altick saw every poetic gesture as necessary to the play's verbal and thematic integrity. Key words such as *earth*, *blood*, *tears*, and *tongue* develop strands of thematic associations, and these strands 'frequently ... cross to form new images. There is no extended passage of the text which is not tied in with the rest of the play by the occurrence of one or more of the familiar symbols' (p. 359). Formalist criticism such as that represented by Altick – as well as by the work of critics such as Madeline Doran (1942), Arthur Suzman (1956), Kathryn Harris (1970), and Karl Felsen (1972) – has changed a great deal over the past 60 years, most notably in its desire to strike a productive balance between aesthetic and political concerns. Nevertheless, Altick's interest in the play's densely textured language, and in the way the play thematizes the power words have not only to 'hypnotize, suspend the sense of reality', but also to 'sting and corrupt' (p. 351) has been fundamental to a wide range of critical approaches. Terence Hawkes (1969), Stephen Booth (1977), Harry Berger, Jr (1987, 1989), Paula Blank (1997), James Siemon (2002), and Madhavi Menon (2003a), critics with markedly different critical and ideological orientations, have all been concerned with the way in which form gives shape to meaning in a play whose central character is preoccupied not only with the external, formalized signs of power, but also with expressing himself poetically.

Madhavi Menon's essay '*Richard II* and the taint of metonymy' is a vivid example of both the evolution away from the more purely aesthetic criticism of Altick, and the endurance of that aesthetic criticism's principles. The chief aim of Menon's argument is to dismantle and expose the underlying assumptions of literary criticism that has located Richard's weakness in his ineffectual verbosity. For Menon, as for Altick, the center of the argument, and indeed the play, is the garden scene (III.iv), a scene that is typically read metaphorically, where the overgrowth of the garden is a figure for Richard's wasteful excesses in ceremony and language. But in Menon's view, this metaphorical reading is 'insufficiently accusatory' in that the crime it expresses is merely one of language – Richard falling prey to, failing to see through, the flattering words of counselors such as Bushy, Bagot, and Green. In order fully to understand the garden scene's indictment of Richard, Menon argues, one must read the Gardener's speech metonymically – an effect given in place of an unspoken cause. To locate the unspoken cause, one must put the Gardener's speech into dialogue with other moments of excess in the play: Bolingbroke's accusation that Bushy and Green have 'Broke the possession of a royal bed / And stained the beauty of a fair queen's cheeks / With tears, drawn from her eyes by your foul wrongs' (III.i.13–15); and perhaps the only moment in the play where the extremity of Richard's emotions overcomes his verbal control, III.ii.121–7, when he hears that his friends have been captured and killed by Bolingbroke. These isolated moments, where we see clearly but briefly Richard's passionate attachment to his male flatterers, can be seen, like weeds in a garden, as unchecked and dangerous outgrowths upon the orderly surface of the play's political narrative. These passages in conjunction with the garden scene suggest that Richard's crime

> is that neither his language nor his sexuality is metaphoric enough, that he fails to realize both the value of words and the worth of heterosexuality.…While criticism has seized eagerly on the failing of excessive verbosity, it has tended to ignore the echo of this excess in the King's sexuality…The alternative reading of the garden scene suggests a metonymic corruption not immediately visible, even as it is everywhere present; it feeds accusations that are made metaphorically, but whose criminality lies in their metonymic detail. (p. 669)

Menon's concern with homosexual subtext and with the ideological evasions of the critical tradition are not concerns we find in mid-century formalist criticism. However, the way in which she develops her argument out of intricate verbal parallels, working toward a densely layered interpretation of the garden scene as dramatizing a 'universe in which weedy vice is screened by the flower of royal language' (p. 668) gives us a vision of the play that is at least as 'symphonic' and coherent as that of Altick and the close readers who followed him.

Performance criticism: the king's many bodies

Coleridge, as I noted above, did not think *Richard II* could work on the stage: no actor is 'capable' of performing the role as Shakespeare has conceived it in all its variegated extremes. Like many of his romantic contemporaries, Coleridge went around the problem of Richard's theatricality by interpreting the character as a figure for the poet and the poetic mind; while Coleridge's view that the play is unperformable has been out of fashion for some time, the legacy of his interpretation of Richard as a figure for the poet has been the extensive formalist tradition discussed above. The modern performance tradition seems to have convincingly disproved Coleridge's claim that there is no actor capable of representing Richard: the play is relatively popular among the histories, and the title role has been taken on by all of the twentieth century's greatest Shakespearean actors. Nevertheless, the play has generated relatively little performance *criticism*. R. F. Hill (1961) was perhaps one of the first to use an idea of performance to take the beauties of the play's poetry beyond the boundaries of the page: his essay imagines the play's 'highly self-conscious and mannered language' (p. 101) from the perspective of a playwright interested in rhetorical rather than naturalistic modes of representation. Hill still saw *Richard II* in Coleridge's terms, however, as a qualified theatrical success. This perspective gradually came to be modified over the next 30 years in, for example, the work of Leonard Barkan (1978), whose theatrical interpretation worked to make sense of what seem, on the page, to be tonal incongruities – specifically the surprisingly comic moments such as the second gauge scene and the York scenes in act five; and Phyllis Rackin (1985), who presented an influentially complex picture of the characterization of York from a theatrical audience's point of view. More recently, a number of performance histories, and studies similar to the present one, have used *Richard II*'s modern performance tradition as a starting point for the interpretation of the text: see Page (1987), Hakola (1988), Shewring (1996), and the authors cited below. In this emergent performance criticism, Richard is no longer construed as a figure for the poet and the process of poetic creation, but rather as a figure for the playwright and the craft of acting.

Richard II has had the good fortune (or bad fortune, depending on your point of view – this is an issue to be discussed in the next chapter) of two highly innovative, controversial productions that have made their way into the scholarly discourse. The earlier of these is John Barton's 1973 Royal Shakespeare Company production with Richard Pasco and Ian Richardson alternating in the roles of Richard and Bolingbroke (discussed in Chapter 5). Both Scott McMillin (1984) and Carol Rutter (1997) have analyzed this production in their discussions of *Richard II*'s theatrical mirroring of Bolingbroke and Richard. For McMillin, the mirroring of these roles in Barton's production was an attempt to solve a problem – the external representation of interiority – that Shakespeare's play actually refuses to solve: Barton's Bolingbroke came to resemble his Richard, and this allowed the stage to give physical embodiment to Richard's experience of loss; but Shakespeare's Bolingbroke and Richard, according to McMillin, pursue 'quite different paths' after the deposition, and even in the deposition scene, their final scene together, 'their attitudes, the one tight-lipped and watchful, the other rhapsodic and tearful, convey no hint that Bullingbroke mirrors the agony within Richard' (p. 45).

While both McMillin and Rutter saw Barton's production to be brilliant and important, Rutter's discussion of it might be said to give more credence to its theatrical reading of the play's thematic concern with Bolingbroke and Richard as doubles. Rutter understood Barton's doubling in terms of the play's preoccupation with the relationships and conflicts between royal (performed) identity and personal (interior) identity: 'By doubling and alternating the roles of Richard and Bolingbroke, John Barton made doubleness the play's organizing metaphor but then went on to intensify its reference by using it to explore the metaphor of the player-king. What Richard knows and Bolingbroke learns is that to play the king is to play a part' (p. 337). Rutter's discussion of Barton is part of a larger discussion of the second controversial production of *Richard II*, Deborah Warner's 1995 National Theatre production starring Fiona Shaw as the king – also discussed more recently by Elizabeth Klett (2006). For both Rutter and Klett, Warner's radical cross-casting allowed her production to represent more complexly an identity problem that has traditionally been construed as a simple opposition between the masculine (strong) role monarchy demands Richard play and the fundamentally effeminate (weak) nature he cannot overcome. Whereas in other productions, Rutter says, 'the effeminate king was deviant, abnormal', in Warner's, the fact

> that a woman was playing a king without impersonating a man or male behavior meant that the audience saw a Richard who was androgynous rather than effeminate, whose 'womanishness' was not deviant but integral and resonant, inscribing within the role an alternative personal and political orientation. In this production, tears belonged to Richard as 'naturally' as rage did. (1997, p. 318)

For both Klett and Rutter, Warner's production was a necessary shot in the arm for entrenched critical and theatrical thinking about the play *and also* a rediscovery of something fundamental and essential about the play itself. The insistent, alienating metatheatricality of the production, in the words of Fiona Shaw, allowed it to represent Richard's discovery 'that the whole thing has been a complete illusion. There isn't anything *real* about being a king' (quoted in Klett, p. 185). 'The theme of acting', Klett goes on to say, 'is connected with Richard's identity crisis once he has been deposed: bereft of the role that has defined him, he must start to discover himself, moving from god-like ruler to all-too-human "nothing".'

Textual scholarship and editing: making the text

Coherent as modern criticism and performance have found *Richard II*'s poetry to be, they have to a certain extent had to construct this coherence out of a notably fragmented text. As discussed in Chapter 1, the lines in which Richard gives his crown to Bolingbroke (corresponding to the Signet edition's IV.i.154–317) appear for the first time in the 1608 Quarto text, 11 years after the play's first printing. Moreover, these 164 'new' or 'previously missing' lines appear in a slightly different form in the 1623 Folio edition. Textual scholars and editors have been industrious in positing theories about the provenance and authority of the play's various versions: the best summary of the modern editorial tradition is in Charles R. Forker's Arden edition of 2002 (see Further Reading for a list of other recent editions of the play). The general editorial consensus is that the

1597 Quarto was probably printed from Shakespeare's manuscript, or a transcript of that manuscript – possibly censored or edited for printing or performance, depending on one's view of the political import of IV.i (see below). The Folio text, scholars generally agree, was probably printed from a copy of the 1598 Quarto that had been annotated with reference to the prompt-book – the text, that is, specially constructed for use during theatrical performance; that is why the Folio's stage directions tend to be more detailed. That prompt-book (of which no copy is extant – indeed, the very existence of a prompt-book is mainly a hypothesis) might have been a transcript of Shakespeare's manuscript, perhaps including the deposition scene, and quite possibly modified to meet various theatrical exigencies in the period between the play's sixteenth-century premiere and the publication of the 1623 Folio. It is plain to see, in light of this condensed textual history, any critical interpretation of *Richard II* as a 'whole' that includes the deposition scene is necessarily based on a potentially chaotic or self-contradictory assembly of (sometimes missing or even imaginary) parts.

The effect the fragmented nature of one of the crucial moments in *Richard II*'s text might have upon detailed formalist readings can be demonstrated vividly with one small example. Looking into a mirror in the Signet edition's version of IV.i, Richard wonders,

> Was this face the face
> That every day under this household roof
> Did keep ten thousand men? Was this the face
> That, like the sun, did make beholders wink?
> Was this the face that faced so many follies,
> And was at last outfaced by Bolingbroke?

(pp. 280–5)

These lines are an allusion to and appropriation of a famous line from Christopher Marlowe's *Doctor Faustus*, the moment when Faustus sees the image of Helen of Troy, called up before him by his servant-devils: 'Was this the face that launched a thousand ships?' In his dazzling analysis of this and the scene's other Marlovian echoes, Harry Berger, Jr (1989) sees Richard responding to his downfall by 'relentlessly' pursuing 'the image of an actor in the Marlovian mode' (p. 67). Cursing Northumberland as a 'Fiend' who 'torments me ere I come to hell' (line 269), Richard's echo of Marlowe 'mocks itself, in part because [he] acknowledges his crimes and sins even as he inflates – or reduces – Northumberland to one of the powers of darkness that control his fate' (p. 68).

> In Richard's little Marlovian tragedy the followers who earned their keep with shows of service ... and sunstruck awe were his tempters and (mis)leaders ... The face the mirror shows is itself the reflection of their folly in thus beguiling such a ruler as he knows himself to be. (p. 69)

Was the resonance Berger attributes, and other critics have attributed, to these lines felt by audiences in 1595–6? If, due to censorship, or to the fact that Shakespeare had not yet written these lines, does the 1608 text provide a 'better' or 'richer' experience? Would Shakespeare, clearly responding in his play to Marlowe's relatively recent *Edward II* (1592), have more likely hit upon this rich construction at an early stage (thus making the censorship hypothesis more likely), or would he have had to develop into it (thus making the revision hypothesis more likely)? And might we see the fact that *Doctor Faustus* was published for the first time in 1604 as a potentially significant factor in Shakespeare's hypothetical revision of his own text?

But even if we were to come to a definite decision about the relationship between Q 1608 and Q 1597 – to be satisfied that both contained the allusion to Marlowe, or that only one did – there would still be further, even more minute concerns pressing upon interpretation. This is what the passage looks like in the 1608 text:

> Was this the face that euery day vnder his
> Houshould roofe did keepe ten thousand men?
> Was this the face that faast so many follies,
> And was at last outfaast by *Bullingbrooke*?

And this is how it appears in the 1623 Folio:

> Was this Face, the Face
> That euery day, vnder his House-hold Roofe,
> Did keepe ten thousand men? Was this the Face,
> That like the Sunne, did make beholders winke?
> Is this the Face, which fac'd so many follyes,
> That was at last out-fac'd by *Bullingbrooke*?

Comparing these two passages to the passage as it appears in the Signet reveals quite strikingly the way in which the creation of a modern text of *Richard II*, and the creation of interpretations founded upon these texts, is a somewhat Frankensteinian labour. The Signet edition, which operates under the assumption that the Folio provides the best text of the abdication scene, uses Folio's lineation of the passage, and its extra line and a half. While it replaces the final line's *That* with Q 1608's *And*, it retains Folio's *was at last outfaced*, presumably because it is metrically more elegant. But, perhaps most significantly, the Signet edition accepts 1608's final 'Was this the face' rather than Folio's '*Is* this the face?' The logic of this final decision is, presumably, to maintain the poetic parallelism, the deliberately resounding echo of Marlowe, in the repeated construction *Was this*. But perhaps the 1623 Folio represents, as its compilers claimed, the 'True Originall' version of Shakespeare's text in this case. Perhaps what Shakespeare wanted here was an alienating shift in syntax; perhaps he wanted to break the hypnotic spell of familiar Marlovian poetry, slightly old fashioned in its beauty, and in so doing to represent a moment of terrifying epiphany for Richard, where the pleasures of nostalgic self-pity give way to a stark awareness of his situation in the present moment. (Berger's analysis, I should note here, is based on a text that gives *Is* rather than *Was*.) The difference between *was* and *is* is merely a matter of two letters, but choosing which of these letters to use and which to relegate to the editorial apparatus is potentially as consequential a decision as that an actor makes when he chooses to represent Richard as a tyrant or a victim.

Playing and politics: *Richard II*, the Essex revolt, and historical criticism

Textual editing and the reconstruction of an authoritative text have interpretive ramifications beyond the realm of formal analysis. Throughout the past century, and especially since the late 1970s, critics have been energetically concerned with using the story of the 'missing' 164 lines in IV.i as an illustrative example of Shakespeare's political engagement – or lack thereof – through his drama. Without these lines, IV.i might be said simply to represent a usurpation that is clearly illegal: the Bishop of Carlisle is summarily arrested after giving eloquent voice to the principle of divine right (IV.i.114–49), and the fact that Richard is not on the stage can give York's announcement that he has 'with willing soul' adopted Bolingbroke as his heir (IV.i.107–10) a decidedly hollow ring. Richard's absence here, that is, might be an effective device by means of which to increase an audience's sympathy for him and for the idea of divine right. If, on the other hand, the scene is performed as it appears in the Folio, it might take on a dangerously inflammatory character; in the longer version of the scene Richard might be said to do nothing but prove that he *is* unfit to rule, might be said to be entirely complicit in his own deposition. This is not to say that putting Richard on stage in this scene would necessarily make Bolingbroke more sympathetic than Richard; Bolingbroke can still come across as a thug who has coerced Richard into giving up much more than he ever claimed he would. But representing two such unsympathetic characters on stage, fighting over the crown, might be the most effective way of dramatizing a highly cynical view of the principle of divine right: neither man is really fit to rule, and the means by which one or the other will become or remain king is simply a matter of brute strength. Critics interested in the historical and political circumstances of *Richard II*'s production, both in 1597 and after, have worked to use interpretations such as these in conjunction with documentary historical evidence in order to argue for an authoritative text of the play, a narrative justifying its authority, and the place of that text in Elizabethan and Jacobean political discourse.

For some critics, such as David Bergeron (1974), the simplest explanation for the difference between Q 1597 and Q 1608 is the most likely: since there is no evidence of censorship in the 1597 text, and since no printed text before 1608 contains the missing lines, Shakespeare probably did not write the scene until sometime around the 1608 printing. Janet Clare (1990), on the other hand, has called attention to the way in which the scene makes sense without the missing lines, and has suggested that Shakespeare might have deliberately written something inflammatory, to see how much he could get away with, fully expecting the passage to be excised by the Master of the Revels. Clare suggests another censorship possibility as well, which was elaborated later and in more detail by Cyndia Susan Clegg (1997): the play might have been *performed* in its entirety – as it appears, that is, in the Folio text – but might have

been censored by the ecclesiastical authorities who were responsible
for licensing *printed* matter for publication. What is at stake in this
debate is the degree to which the 164 lines in IV.i can be seen as deliberately inflammatory or subversive. Bergeron thinks that the lines
are *not* subversive, and in fact that when they are performed in the
theatre they *increase* our sympathy for Richard and our sense that
Bolingbroke's usurpation is unjust. Clare imagines that the scene
might not have seemed too subversive in the context of the public
theatre – an institution that had a unique license to speak relatively
freely, on the understanding that this license was limited to the
space and time of the theatrical event; for Clare, the permanence
of print might have made the scene more dangerous, made it part
of a group of contemporaneously produced subversive writings
in which analogies between Richard II and Queen Elizabeth were
made. Clegg makes a similar argument, connecting *Richard II* with
a censored 1595 work, Robert Parsons's *A Conference upon the Next
Succession*, which, among other things, argues that the deposition
of Richard II was legitimate because it occurred by parliamentary
process; the representation of parliamentary process, Clegg argues,
is what an audience sees if Richard is allowed to come on stage in
this scene.

It should be pointed out here that *Richard II* is by no means the
only one of Shakespeare's plays to exist in different versions. In
most of his plays, in fact, there are significant differences between
Quarto and Folio texts, and/or between one Quarto and another.
Such textual variation has not in every case sparked debate about the
political and ideological stakes of theatrical production in the early
modern period; there are hundreds of small differences between the
1622 *Othello* Quarto and the Folio text of that play, and many of these
clearly have to do with the revision of a copy text that had been produced prior to a 1606 Act of Parliament forbidding religious oaths
on stage. But *Othello* is not generally, as *Richard II* is, discussed as a
representative instance of the potentially antagonistic relationship
between government and the theatre. The reason for the difference
has to do both with the fact that the evidence is much more difficult
to interpret in the case of *Richard II*, and with the fact that the issue
around which theatre and government may or may not have converged in *Richard II* was much more explosive than simply taking the
Lord's name in vain on the stage.

To elaborate upon some information given briefly above in Chapter 1: on 8 February 1601, Robert Devereux, the Earl of Essex, having been disgraced by Elizabeth I for his failure in and premature return from a military campaign in Ireland, mounted an ill-fated rebellion against the Queen; having drastically miscalculated popular support for his uprising, Essex, marching toward the palace, found the city gates locked and heavily guarded and so retreated to his house, where he was then forced to surrender by the Earl of Nottingham. Within ten days, Essex had been condemned of treason, and in another week, on 25 February 1601, he was beheaded. Virtually every step in this sequence of events – from Essex's unexpected return in 1599 and surprise appearance in the Queen's bedchamber, to his plotting rebellion while under house arrest, to his abortive uprising, to his stoicism at his execution – can be, and has been, seen as political theatre of the highest order. Political theatre and commercial theatre converged around this incident when, on 7 February 1601, the eve of the Essex revolt, the Lord Chamberlain's Men were paid by supporters of Essex to perform a play about Richard II. Whether or not this play about Richard II performed on 7 February was *Shakespeare's* is of course uncertain, but the fact remains that the playing company for which he worked came into close, perhaps even dangerous proximity with one of the great political dramas of Elizabeth's reign. Indeed, one of Shakespeare's fellow players, Augustine Philips, was called before the Lord Chief Justice to explain the company's actions. At the same time, as I have noted in Chapter 1, the play about Richard II performed on 7 February notably did *not* rouse the city against the Queen. The testimony of Philips reveals that the company itself might have thought from the start that such an out-of-date play was unlikely to excite anyone at all.

Using *Richard II* as a key text for understanding the relationship between playing and politics in the Elizabethan period has been common critical practice for at least the last century, but it has attained a particular urgency and detail in the last 25 years, with the advent of New Historicist criticism. In his introduction to *The Power of Forms in the English Renaissance* (1982), the book that introduced the term 'new historicism' into the critical lexicon, Stephen Greenblatt used *Richard II* as his keynote text. In his view, *Richard II* is a literary text whose complex interaction with political history made it ideally suited to his collection's critical project of challenging 'the assumptions that guarantee a secure distinction between "literary foreground" and "political background" or, more generally, between artistic production and other kinds of social production' (p. 6). Greenblatt's 'new' historicism was self-consciously formulated in opposition to an earlier historicism that he defined as 'monological ... concerned with discovering a single political vision, usually identical to that said to be held by the entire literate class or indeed the entire population' (p. 5). In such earlier historicist formulations (represented by the work of critics such as J. Dover Wilson and E. M. W. Tillyard), a play like *Richard II* was 'not at all subversive but rather a hymn to Tudor order. ... [F]ar from encouraging thoughts of rebellion, [it] regards the deposition of the legitimate king as a "sacreligious" act ...' (p. 4). In order to make the claim that *Richard II* was genuinely subversive, Greenblatt took for granted that Queen Elizabeth's remark to William Lambard, 'I am Richard II, know ye not that', referred to a recent production of Shakespeare's play, paid for by the Essex conspirators. In the compellingly paradoxical way typical of new historicist formulations, Greenblatt's emphasis on *Richard II*'s subversiveness leads to a corresponding emphasis on the inevitable containment of subversion by amorphous and pervasive forces of institutional authority: 'even before the Essex rising, the actual deposition scene ... *was carefully omitted* from the first three quartos of Shakespeare's play and appears only after Elizabeth's death' (p. 4). The italics in that quotation are my own and are intended to call attention to the way in which Greenblatt's use of the passive voice makes mysterious – and all the more powerful – the forces, very generally linked to the person of the Queen, that set limits upon what the Essex conspirators could expect to achieve even before they attempted it.

From the perspective of new historicist criticism, at least as formulated by Greenblatt (perhaps most influentially in his 1984 *Renaissance Self-fashioning*), the fictions and fantasies of popular culture are licensed to voice powerful social critique. This is precisely because such critique always ultimately re-legitimizes the voice of authority. In this context, the debates about rightful sovereignty and succession that structure the action of *Richard II* can clearly be seen to give voice to, and to control, late sixteenth-century anxieties about the fate of England under an aging Queen, counseled by a tight circle of insiders, who refused to marry. From this perspective, the Essex revolt, which was at least ostensibly about the Queen being led astray by her councilors, could be seen as the manifestation – six years after the play's first performance – of the deep social anxiety to which Shakespeare's histrionic, self-involved king gave voice; and the fact that the Essex revolt was quickly, even easily put down, and that the official word from the players was, 'It was only a play – and an old one at that', could be seen as a demonstration of New Historicism's dictum that all subversion is ultimately contained. Following Greenblatt's lead in seeing the stage as a site for both royal authority and its limits (or limitations) to be represented, critics of the past three decades have energetically debated the place of Shakespeare's play not only in the early modern enterprise of representing medieval English history, but also in the early modern enterprise of theorizing contemporary English nationhood. Such critical approaches have been greatly influenced by Greenblatt's model of new historicism, but also concerned to build upon, revise, and rethink his paradigm of subversion and containment: see, for example, Orgel (1982), Barroll (1988), Pye (1988, 1990), Belsey (1991), Clare (1990), and Clegg (1997), and Fitter (2005).

Coda: the problem of laughter in *Richard II*

Similar to much of the critical analysis of *Richard II* which I have surveyed here, my scene-by-scene analysis in Chapter 2 has made the play seem to be a solemn affair. Critics have generally agreed over the years, both explicitly and through their silence on the matter, that the play is notably devoid of funny moments. The *Variorum* edition contains a substantial paragraph that begins by noting that '*Richard II* contains hardly a trace of [Shakespeare's] humor, and many critics have enlarged on this' (p. 515). A quotation from J. M. Murry's *Shakespeare* (1936) registers the surprising fact that there is no Bastard-like character in *Richard II*, a play closely contemporaneous with *King John*. And T. M. Parrott (*Shakespearean Comedy*, 1949) is quoted saying 'One misses [in *Richard II*] the vigorous dramatic action of Shakespeare's other histories. More especially one feels the absence of comic scenes and comic characters'. In the *Variorum*'s section on the play's style, more than one commentary notes that *Richard II* is among the most carefully controlled Shakespearean plays in terms of its use of wordplay and puns. Certainly the play has many sardonic ironies, both overt and implicit – the timing of Mowbray's death and Bolingbroke's reaction to it (IV.i.86–106), for example, or the perverse

verbal mirroring of Gaunt and Richard in II.i; but episodes that seem
to verge on being overtly comic – the second gauge scene (IV.i.1–85), for
example, or the scenes involving the York family in the play's last act –
have generally been treated as tonally problematic moments for which
one must try to find a solution: much critical and theatrical energy, that
is, has been expended on explaining how the scenes would not have
been comic to Shakespeare's original audience, or how they are only
comic if a modern production does not take them seriously enough,
or how they are sufficiently incongruous with the rest of the action to
justify their excision.

My aim in this final section of the chapter is not to disagree with
this consensus, for I do feel that the play is quite explicitly a solemn,
serious one – one that wrestles, as many critics have noted, in an
extraordinarily poetic way (it is one of only two plays Shakespeare
wrote entirely in verse) not only with deep problems of royal
authority and succession but also with the problem of representing
complex, conflicted interiority. What I seek to do, rather, is to chip
away a little at the play's feeling of intense all-encompassing coherence, a coherence that stifles the incongruities on which laughter
necessarily depends. By putting pressure on the coherences of the
play to such an extent that they reveal their fissures, either in terms
of the structure of the play or the changing conditions of its reception, I hope to make palpable some of the anarchic energies that
the play's rigorous, decorous structures work to keep under control. The discussion that follows will deal with such anarchic energies lying just beyond the grasp of two dominant modes of *Richard
II* criticism: formalist and historical.

One of the most densely coherent passages of poetry in *Richard II*
occurs in his lament upon returning to England and hearing that
Bolingbroke has begun to execute his followers (III.ii.144–77). I am
particularly interested in these four lines:

> Our lands, our lives, and all are Bolingbroke's,
> And nothing can we call our own, but death
> And that small model of the barren earth
> Which serves as paste and cover to our bones.

> (III.ii.151–4)

This short passage is a masterpiece of densely layered, complex
repetition: the parallel structure of line 151, with the two repeated

Ours, makes the phrase *and all are* sound for a moment like *and all our*. The introduction of *Bolingbroke's* at the end of the line carries a listener's understanding in a different direction, but the briefly heard *all our* is echoed in the same metrical position in line 152's *call our*. The anaphora (consecutive lines beginning in the same way) of lines 152 and 153 is an explicit patterning device, and both lines have a subtler echo in the preceding *and all* of line 151. Further, the phrase *and **all*** in line 151 is both echoed and opposed by *And **nothing*** in line 152. The sound of *and all* from line 151 is broken apart and redistributed over the phrases '*can* we c*all*' in line 152 and '*And* that sm*all*' in line 153. The word *model* introduces a new vowel sound into the passage, but does so by means of alliteration: the initial and final consonants of the word echo faintly with the beginning and end of the preceding word, *small*. Alliteration, as well as metrical position and ideational attraction, also draws *death* and *earth* together; the new vowel sound in *paste* juts out with surprising bitterness between the subdued alliterating vs. and closed vowels of *serves* and *cover* in line 154. And line 154's final two words, *our bones*, rattle hollowly together with 152's *our own*. Around the edges of the echo between lines 152 and 154 lies, I think, the hint of a sing-song rhyming structure that might summarize the entire passage: 'and *nothing can* we *call* our *own* / but [this] *paste* and *cover* to our *bones*'.

Appreciating the sonic density of these four lines is easy for the literary critic. Part of that density is obviously consciously created by the poet (the *anaphora*, for example), and part of it is probably the unconscious result of his highly sophisticated poetic ear. It is also easy to construe the poetic density of this passage in thematic terms: at one of the first moments Richard realizes his only recourse will be to abandon all he has, his identity begins to reside wholly in his ability to manipulate, beautifully but hopelessly, the sounds of words. Appreciating the sing-song rhyming structure I have identified as underlying the passage is a little less easy: certainly, it is something an actor might call attention to, but to do so would probably be to call too much attention to the sonic density of the passage generally – it might suggest that the poetry is overwrought, bad, or that the actor is taking more license with the poetry than one would expect the playwright to have desired. Moreover, to read against the smooth grain of the elegantly interlocking words in this passage might have the surprisingly detrimental effect of calling more attention to what the words are *saying* than how they *sound*. As critics at least since Samuel Johnson have noticed with some embarrassment, Richard's metaphor of the *paste* asks his listener to imagine the grave as a pie (for which one familiar word in the Elizabethan period was *coffin*) and the body as its tasty filling. It is hard to see here whether it is Richard alone or Shakespeare as well who is allowing his poetic imagination to get the better of him – allowing the more conventional idea of the grave eating dead flesh to metamorphose in a rather perverse, grotesque way – and hard to see whether an actor is meant to follow or ignore the signals of the poetry, to pursue the exaggerated coherence of the passage. It is also hard to see to what extent Shakespeare pursued the implications of this passage and its submerged play on the two ideas of *coffin* when he came to write the play's final scene, in which the interred Richard – the very image of all he has left – is brought onto the stage: a dainty dish set before the new king.

What I have been suggesting in this brief examination of a particular kind of poetic density – one that I think might safely be said to be characteristic of *Richard II* – is that there is a way in which the coherence critics and audiences so value in the play's language frequently contains the seeds of its own undoing; the proliferation of correspondences between multiple layers of sonic, thematic, and ideational meanings frequently threatens to move beyond the abilities of an actor or interpreter to control: to become, when given its full measure, literally ridiculous, provocative of laughter.

*   *   *

Historical criticism is as interested as formalist criticism in the principle of coherence, and it can be as productively alienating with the former as with the latter to apply a kind of intense pressure to the search for direct parallels. In the case of historical criticism of *Richard II*, the play can only be seen as closely related to the Essex revolt insofar as we can see Richard as an Elizabeth figure (lofty, performative, badly counseled) and Bolingbroke as an Essex figure (dangerously popular, formerly loyal, rebelling in the name of the nation's greater good). We might decide that Shakespeare is equivocal on the matter – that he is as aware of Bolingbroke/Essex's dangerous self-interest as of Elizabeth/Richard's destructive self-involvement, and that he is not necessarily authorizing rebellion so much as analyzing its causes – but we need to decide that the correspondences are there in order to make this decision; we need, that is, to assume that political meanings in art arise out of a linear relationship between the work of art and its historical context.

The difficulty with this approach in the case of *Richard II* is that the historical timeline and the timeline of the play's publication and performance do not work together entirely conveniently. In 1595–7, the period when *Richard II* was written, first performed, and first printed, the Earl of Essex was still very much a representative figure of England's national strength – among other things, he was responsible for the capture of Cadiz in 1596. The relationship between Essex and the Queen was never placid, and recently the argument has been made that some of the cultural work *Richard II* might have done in its first performances was to allegorize the threat a strong, popular Essex posed to the heirless Queen (see Fitter 2005). But it is only in the retrospective light cast by the rebellion of 1601, where Essex was both rebel and self-proclaimed hero, that a prophetic equation, in Shakespeare's play, between Essex and Bolingbroke can be seen to be at all vivid. And, most interestingly for my purposes here, the circumstances of the 1601 rebellion were such that they had the potential to yield up political and allegorical resonances significantly different from those that were only vaguely possible in 1595–7.

What I mean is this: what audiences and readers in 1595–7 could not have known was that the catalyst for Essex's revolt four or five years later would be his failure, as Lord Lieutenant of Ireland, to suppress a rebellion there, and his humiliation by the Queen and her council when he returned to England before accomplishing the mission for which he was sent. It would be somewhat of an exaggeration to say that everything changed for Essex when he went to Ireland, but a spectator at the Globe on 7 February 1601, if he or she was watching Shakespeare's play, and if he or she had some sense that the performance had been paid for by Essex's supporters, might certainly have found a humorously coincidental irony in the fact that, as with Essex, Richard's biggest mistake was going to Ireland. Like Shakespeare's Richard, the Earl of Essex left for Ireland with great fanfare; like Shakespeare's Richard, the Earl of Essex was unsuccessful in suppressing the rebellion he set out to suppress; like Shakespeare's Richard, the Earl of Essex returned desperately to an England that would no longer accommodate him. Our hypothetical spectator in 1601, lured to the theatre by the promise of controversy but perhaps not committed one way or the other to Essex's cause, might indeed have had to stifle a guilty chuckle as he or she noted the correspondences between Richard and Essex, and wondered if Essex and his friends had simply forgotten about the importance of Richard's Irish adventure when they commissioned Shakespeare's old play.

Of course, a Richard-Essex parallel is implausible, and Bolingbroke-Elizabeth merely fanciful. My point here is that the direct-parallels game, and the construction of a linear relationship between history and art, often only goes as far as proving the point the critic hoped to prove before he or she set out finding the parallels. History, like poetic language, is always much more chaotic than criticism can bear; plays, especially popular ones like Shakespeare's, accrue meanings over time, as they are viewed by different audiences and under different circumstances; all the evidence suggests that sixteenth-century readers and spectators could have perceived energetic relationships between Shakespeare's play and contemporary political crises, but all the evidence suggests that the ways in which they perceived those relationships, or the relationships they perceived, were heterogeneous, complicated, and frequently contradictory. Shakespeare's plays, of course, continue to be viewed, and under circumstances almost completely alien to those under which they were first written, performed, and viewed; and they continue to accrue new meanings, as we will see in the next chapter, both because and in spite of the best efforts of actors, directors, audiences, and critics.

5 Key Productions and Performances

Mark Rylance – Globe Theatre, 2003

One of the most interesting and unexpected developments in the parallel worlds of Shakespearean theatre and scholarship at the end of the twentieth century and the beginning of the twenty-first century has been the resurgent interest in 'original practices' – in scholarship that uncovers information, and theatrical productions that make use of that information, about the physical conditions that governed theatrical performance in the late sixteenth and early seventeenth centuries. The rationale behind original practices as a theatrical methodology is that Shakespeare and his contemporaries were intimately familiar with the theatrical buildings, and the spatial dynamics of the buildings, in which their plays would have been performed; if modern theatrical productions of early modern theatrical texts are to do justice to those texts, it is necessary to strip away many centuries of accrued conventions – the proscenium arch, the imaginary 'fourth wall', the darkened theatre, and the passive audience – and allow the plays to speak from within a physical space that approximates that for which they were originally written. The crowning monument of this movement is the new Shakespeare's Globe Theatre, a reconstruction of the 1599 Globe; this reconstruction opened on the south bank of the Thames river in 1997.

But the idea of a return to the 'basics' of early modern theatrical performance is not a new one: its late nineteenth- and early twentieth-century champion was the actor and theatrical manager William Poel, whose belief in the importance of Elizabethan staging conventions for the production of Elizabethan plays was largely a reaction against the excesses of the 'pictorial' staging conventions of the Victorian theatre. Important descendants of Poel in the first half of the twentieth century in England included Harley Granville-Barker and Tyrone Guthrie, who believed in the importance of an open stage that facilitated swift movement in the production of early modern drama. Largely by means of Guthrie, who helped to found the Stratford Festival of Canada in Stratford, Ontario in 1955, the 'original practices' movement migrated to North America. At the time the Stratford Festival was founded, however, a version of 'original practices' had already been in operation for some time at the Oregon Shakespeare Festival in Ashland, Oregon. Founded in 1935 by Angus L. Bowmer, who noticed the similarity between the walls of a local, abandoned domed building and an Elizabethan theatre, the Festival constructed an 'Elizabethan stage' in 1947, and a new one in 1959. Other north American analogues include the San Diego Old Globe Theatre (also built in 1935) and the Globe of the Great Southwest in Odessa, Texas (built in 1968). The most important recent original practices project is the reconstruction of the *indoor* theatre for which Shakespeare wrote in the last years of his career: the American Shakespeare Center's Blackfriars Theatre, reconstructed in Staunton, Virginia, opened in 2001.

Shakespeare's Globe Theatre in London is, both by design and of necessity, the most thoroughgoing original practices theatre in the world. Located some 200 meters from the site of the original Globe, painstakingly crafted from the materials – oak beams, plaster walls, thatched roof – and according to the methods that would have been available to sixteenth-century craftsmen, and in the heart of a major international tourist destination that is famous for both its history and its theatre, the new Globe has the privilege (and bears the burden) of representing something authentic and fundamental about the Shakespearean theatrical experience. According to the theatre's website, it seeks with its 'faithfully reconstructed Globe Theatre' to 'appeal to the widest spectrum of visitors', and to achieve an 'international reputation for performance excellence through its productions...in performance conditions reproducing those of Shakespeare's time'. Those performing conditions include an opulent, open-air wooden theatre whose huge stage thrusts out into a pit capable of holding 700 standing spectators; three tiers of gallery seating; lavish Elizabethan costuming, often made from the fabrics and according to methods that would have been available to Elizabethan clothiers; incidental music played on period instruments; and a fast-paced, semi-naturalistic, highly interactive playing style, the aim of which is to make the exalted classics of English drama come alive in surprising and unpretentious ways. The Globe's production of *Richard II* – performed in repertory with *Richard III*, *Taming of the Shrew*, and Marlowe's *Dido* and *Edward II* during the 2003 season – in many ways embodied all the elements that constitute an original practices performance, and all the effects such a performance seeks to achieve.

The part of Richard was played by Mark Rylance, artistic director at the Globe through the 2005 season. His interpretation of the character, which was very popular with critics and audiences alike, was idiosyncratic and unusual, but quite typical of the work for which Rylance had become known at the Globe. Actors playing Richard always have the opportunity to surprise the audience with a few moments of bitter humour – in the King's reaction to Gaunt's death ('So much for that'), for example, or his mischievous response to Bolingbroke's demand whether he is willing to resign the crown ('Ay, no, no ay'). But no actor that I have seen or read about in the role has been able to provoke quite so much laughter as Rylance; his ability to do so derived largely from his peculiar verbal delivery that took advantage of the Globe audiences's willingness to be engaged.

A representative example of this delivery style can be seen in Rylance's handling of what is traditionally thought of as a highly lyrical scene, III.ii, when Richard returns to England and begins to realize that it no longer belongs to him. After beginning by indulging fully the heroic tone with which Richard's salutation of his land begins (III.ii.4–17), Rylance abruptly undercut that tone with bathetic theatrical business: on the line 'Yield stinging nettles to mine enemies' (III ii.18), he moved to the front of the stage, mischievously holding out to spectators – now his 'enemies' – pieces of foliage that he had brought on at the beginning of the scene. The surprised, delighted laughter this provoked – especially among those who were the recipients of or able clearly to see the business – meant that, to a large extent, Richard could never be seen as having been *forced* to give up his kingdom: he had given it up even before arriving from Ireland, and was content now in taking on the role of his own court jester.

At the same time, it is important to note that Rylance's extremely agile vocal style allowed him quickly, if momentarily, to hush the audience's laughter and suggest that there was something more at stake for Richard than performing a loss he had already accepted. Such was the feeling of III.ii.145–54 ('Let's talk of graves, of worms, and epitaphs...'), before Rylance again pulled the rug out from under his listeners, and deadpanned lines 155–6, 'For God's sake let us sit upon the ground / And tell sad stories of the death of kings', as he plopped abruptly down on the stage floor. As Michael Billington of *The Guardian* wrote, 'Rylance has such vocal virtuosity that at times he seems to be toying with the text' (15 May 2003). Billington went on in his review to discuss another traditionally lyrical moment from which Rylance derived an unexpected laugh: III.iii.152–3, '[I'll give] my large kingdom for a little grave, / A little, little grave, an obscure grave.' Rather than ringing the repetitions of these lines like solemn bells that announce a king's demise, Rylance's Richard said 'my large kingdom for a little grave', and then paused. 'A little, *little* grave', he said, almost as a wry afterthought. Another pause. And then, openly acknowledging the theatrical audience that was, like him, caught up in his ability simply to generate words, 'an *obscure* grave'. The laugh that this halting, highly self-referential and at the same time outwardly directed delivery generated allowed lines 154–8, in which Richard imagines being buried in a place where the maximum amount of traffic can trample upon his head, to be delivered rapidly – as an almost absurd and certainly ridiculous fantasy generated both by his own self-pity and Bolingbroke's ruthlessness.

Billington called the laugh Rylance generated in III.iii 'extraneous' and in a way I am – and was, as a spectator – inclined to agree. I could also add a number of moments about which I am, and was, inclined to think something similar: the reimagining of I.i as a deer-hunting expedition that was interrupted by John of Gaunt, who had had to seek out Richard in order to remind him of the important business at hand (this in turn provided Rylance with the opportunity to establish his comically halting, slightly bemused vocal delivery from the very first line); Richard's farcical attacking of the sick John of Gaunt with a bouquet of flowers in II.i; and the way Rylance said 'That jade!' – in an exasperated tone reminiscent of bewildered protagonists in television comedies – upon hearing from the Groom how his former horse had allowed Bolingbroke to ride him (V.v.85). A survey of both academic and press reviews yields multiple other such instances. But a survey of press reviews *also* demonstrates that Rylance's comedic strategy was overwhelmingly successful – critics found him 'mesmerizing' (Kate Stratton, *Time Out*, 21 May 2003), 'touching and dignified' (Lloyd Evans, *Spectator*, 17 May 2003), and capable of achieving an 'extraordinary quiet intimacy with the audience' (Paul Taylor, *Independent*, 16 May 2003). There was general agreement that the comedic approach surprisingly and fittingly allowed both actor and character to use 'humor for self-distracting protection' and to draw 'laughter from the jaws of grief' in a powerful and uplifting way (Nicholas de Jongh, *Evening Standard*, 15 May 2003). The audience during the performance I saw (in July 2003) seemed to bear out the reviewers' perceptions. To a great extent one must refuse to take a Globe performance on its own terms if one is to argue that the laughs generated by Rylance – which were anchored in, if not always evidently contiguous with, the text – were 'extraneous'.

The terms on which this Globe production worked (and, indeed, on which most Globe productions work) were transparently, ingenuously, and in many ways refreshingly literal. In the early modern theatre, the works of Shakespeare had not yet attained their reverent cultural place, and scholarly research indicates that there was much more interaction between audience and stage – people might well have laughed during the original *Richard II* because they had come to the theatre to enjoy themselves; therefore, the Globe seeks out every opportunity to desacralize Shakespeare, seeks out every opportunity to interact with the audience. One critic complained that Rylance's ironic and free attitude toward the language and the audience trivialized the problems of kingship with which the play is concerned, and ultimately left one 'thinking more about the player than the king' (Ian Johns, *The Times*, 17 May 2003); Rylance would presumably reply that this was entirely the point. In the early modern theatre, the roles of women were played by young boys, and scholarly research has suggested that the performance of female roles on the early modern stage would have very much involved the self-conscious *performance* of femininity rather than any attempt to achieve physical or psychological verisimilitude; therefore, the female characters in the Globe's all-male productions – as this *Richard II* was – are elaborately made up, and walk, gesture, and speak in a highly stylized, frequently stereotyped, and occasionally quite extravagant manner. (The female characters in *Richard II* were the least well-received in the press.) The early modern theatre was more of an actors' theatre than a playwrights', and scholarly research indicates that one important pleasure of the play going experience was that of seeing, and recognizing the style of, familiar actors in diverse roles; therefore Rylance's idiosyncratic vocal delivery in *Richard II* was in large part a means of cultivating his reputation for a particular acting style at the Globe – a style that was also central to his portrayal of *Cymbeline*'s Cloten (2001), *Twelfth Night*'s Olivia (2002), *Measure for Measure*'s Duke (2004), and *Tempest*'s Prospero. As with its thatched roof (the only thatched roof allowed in London since the Great Fire of 1666), its costumes and musical instruments, and its observation of the Elizabethan convention of ending every performance with an exuberant dance, the dramaturgy at the Globe delights in reconstruction for its own sake; one spectator's frustration with a self-trivializing, Chaplin-esque Richard is another's surprised pleasure, and both arise in response to the Globe's challenge that we look at Shakespeare in a new way.

The one thing the Globe cannot reconstruct is an Elizabethan audience, and it is on this point that some of the Globe's 'own terms' can be seen as somewhat inadequate for judging the success and value of a production. For the 2003 *Richard II*, the notorious second gage scene, at the beginning of IV.i, presented no tonal difficulties: Rylance/Richard, the acting company as a whole, and through them the audience, were committed over the course of the performance to discovering laughter and irony in even the most apparently lyrical or tragic moments, and this would be no exception. Refusing to treat Shakespeare's text as a sacred text freed the Globe company from the worries that have plagued directors, scholars, and theatre critics in this scene for at least 100 years. What is more, the Globe production not only sought laughter in this scene – trusting its audience to see the way in which power struggles in this play amounted to a futile and sometimes bitterly comic game – but in fact *included* the audience *in* the scene: at lines 83–5, with the stage already covered in gloves, the now gageless Aumerle turned to the spectators in the yard as he cried 'Some honest Christian trust me with a gage!' After a very few seconds of bewilderment and reticence, some honest Christian standing near the front of the stage handed Aumerle his baseball cap, which Aumerle promptly threw down upon the stage in response to Fitzwater's challenge. The audience was overjoyed with this moment; the arbitrary nature of a quarrel Bolingbroke has no intention of allowing to go any further was expressed theatrically by quite literally bringing the spectators into the world of the play.

But what place does a baseball cap have in a painstakingly recon-structed theatrical experience – one that even goes so far as to cast men in the roles of women? Is there not a tension between asking an audience to be deeply impressed by original fabrics and musical instruments, but to revel in its temporal and ironic distance from medieval and early modern conventions of single combat? While an early modern audience might certainly have seen the absurdity of Aumerle's situation, it also would have understood the serious-ness both of the accusations being made, and the *way* they were bring made. Is it not possible that in this moment the Globe company was not transcending the 'problem' of the second gage scene, but was in fact over-compensating for its difficulty – mistaking laughter for engagement and, consequently, sacrificing an intelligible rendering of the issues at stake in the scene and the play? As was indicated by the Globe production's extensive use of heraldic music, its beautiful ceremonial costumes, its erection of a 'lists' for I.iii, and many other visual details as well, *Richard II* is a very much a play about ritual, and the investment of kings and subjects in the power of ritual. One of the foremost problems with staging *Richard II* in the twenty-first century is that of making an audience feel that ritual is as important as the play suggests it is. The Globe's production often succeeded in doing this by asking the audience to invest in the power of the ritual of Elizabethan theatre-going; but it also occasionally failed by insist-ing that the audience not only engage with a reconstructed theatri-cal experience, but also play a role it was not born to play.

Fiona Shaw – National Theatre, 1995

Twentieth- and twenty-first-century directors, like twentieth- and twenty-first-century literary critics, routinely represent *Richard II* as a play that has, since its earliest productions, courted controversy. But even if one whole-heartedly accepts that the circumstantial evidence connects Shakespeare's play with the Essex conspiracy, understanding the play as controversial requires today's director, actor, or spectator to undertake a significant leap of the imagination, or leap of faith: for, the thing the play seems to subvert is something with which most contemporary directors, actors, and spectators have very little actual experience – namely, the idea of monarchical authority as sanctified and absolute. If the contemporary critic or director accepts that Shakespeare uses the figure of Richard II to comment upon both powerful if defunct medieval ideals of kingship *and* the nostalgic preservation of those ideals in the cult of Elizabeth I – ideals that have long since fallen out of cultural circulation – then he or she cannot carry out Shakespeare's project of undercutting those ideals without first attempting to build them up again. The problem confronting the contemporary director attempting to sell *Richard II* as galvanizing and subversive is, then, a problem of making the audience feel like kingship matters – of making the movement of the play one in which the spectators, like Richard, discover, to their terror, that the identity of a king is merely an illusion.

It is a hard question whether any contemporary production has succeeded in solving this problem. Many productions attempt to address the problem through program notes. The program notes for the 1990 Royal Shakespeare Company production, directed by Ron Daniels, used photographs and historical information to suggest analogies between Richard's reign – explicitly construed, by means of a selective use of historical sources, as tyrannous – and the reigns of various twentieth-century tyrants: Hitler, Mussolini, Idi Amin, Ceausescu, etc. In large font at the centre of the program's two-page collage of dictators was a quotation from Christopher Hibbert: 'Mussolini would have liked to have been a poet just as Hitler would have liked to have been a great painter – most dictators, it seems, are artists manqués'. Armed with this context, a spectator might have seen Richard's poetic solipsisms – performed with tremendous control by the physically imposing Alex Jennings – as a dangerously perverse form of idealism, the art of language put in service of political domination. Daniels's production, whose set and costume design evoked an eastern-bloc dictatorship, made its analogies particularly explicit, but a large number of productions in the last 20 or 30 years have framed themselves in a more or less similar way. The basic purpose is consistent: to make *Richard II* seem to reflect urgent realities or potentialities of political power in modern society.

Modern productions that attempt to court controversy by making explicit analogies between medieval and contemporary power-politics often do not succeed. Using Shakespeare's texts to reflect or speak to a contemporary historical moment has become so conventional that one can take or leave the analogies on aesthetic rather than politicized grounds: the concept might 'work' (resonate interestingly with Shakespeare's text, appear unified and convincing to a spectator) or 'not work' (seem to stretch Shakespeare's text too far, appear somewhat *ad hoc* in its design), but the critic's obligation to engage with its ideological apparatus is minimal because more or less ingenious conceptual analogies are simply what one expects when attending a Shakespeare play. As many reviewers of both Daniels's production and Stephen Pimlott's similarly modernized 2000 RSC production noted, the differences between Shakespeare's Richard and an eastern European strongman are so pronounced as almost inevitably to trivialize the representation of both; what is gained in terms of urgency of topical *frisson* is balanced out by a corresponding loss in dramatic specificity and seriousness. Thus, perhaps not surprisingly, one of the more genuinely controversial productions of *Richard II* in the modern performance tradition was one that did not rely upon contemporary political analogies, but rather set out to subvert the very notion of dramatic specificity and seriousness that for so many critics and audiences disabled such analogies in other productions: this was Deborah Warner's 1995 production at the National Theatre, starring the Irish actress Fiona Shaw as Richard.

As the program notes for Warner's production insisted, there is a long tradition of famous actresses playing Shakespeare's male leads (for example, both Sarah Siddons and Sarah Bernhardt played Hamlet); but such historical precedent did not, of course, decrease the controversy either before or after the production had opened – nor, presumably, would the director and players have wanted it to. By choosing for her cross-casting experiment a character whom critics and reviewers had comfortably referred to as 'effeminate' for at least a century, Deborah Warner used the theatre to literalize a critical metaphor, and in so doing immediately called forth a whole host of critical anxieties about the relationship between theatre and text, performance and identity. Thus, while the *play* Warner presented on stage was not necessarily any more effective than Daniels's in representing and subverting the mystery of kingship (it was criticized for the same kinds of decontextualized trivialization of the monarch), her *production* was actually quite successful at doing what critics and reviewers always hope a production of *Richard II* will do: it challenged and sought to tear down a sacrosanct ideal its audience could be expected in some part to have brought to the theatre. The only trouble – or the real brilliance, depending on your point of view – was that this sacrosanct ideal had nothing to do with kingship and everything to do with Shakespeare as a playwright and cultural icon.

Perhaps the single most frequently observed (and criticized) theatrical gesture in the production was what Fiona Shaw's Richard did during one of the play's most famous passages, 'For God's sake let us sit upon the ground / And tell sad stories of the death of kings' (III.ii.155–78): he sat upon the ground and, speaking such gloriously poetic lines as 'within the hollow crown / That rounds the mortal temples of a king / Keeps Death his court ...' (III.ii.161–3), sucked his thumb. This moment was consistent with the infantilization of the king throughout the play. Shaw and Warner were quite explicit, both in the production's dramaturgy and in interviews about it in the press, that they wanted to construe the relationship between Bolingbroke and Richard as one that had begun in childhood, and whose destructive patterns in adulthood were a continuation and perversion of their youthful games. From the play's very first lines, which Richard spoke giggling and half-hiding behind the throne, Shaw's characterization was irreverently energetic: her Richard hung upon Bolingbroke's neck at every opportunity, challenging him to push the king away and establish the sovereignty of his personal space. During the deposition scene, Richard taunted Bolingbroke mercilessly with the words 'Ay, no, no, ay', shouting the first syllable with an almost joyful certainty, then running away from Bolingbroke and extending the second: 'Noooooooo!' The next half of the phrase, 'No, ay' was spoken rapidly and almost unconcernedly: no one knew what Richard might do next. Fascinatingly, and surprisingly, what Richard did next, on the lines 'I give this heavy weight from off my head,' etc. (IV.i.203–9), was to *mime* the removal of his crown and the giving over of his sceptre, for at this moment he possessed neither; and indeed, this solemn and moving moment suggested, he never had. The solemnity of the moment did not last long: fewer than 20 lines later, responding to Northumberland's demand that he read out the accusations made against him, Richard was on his knees, pounding the stage with his fists, throwing a childish tantrum: 'Must I do so?' The rapid tonal and physical shifts in this scene were characteristic of Shaw's performance throughout: her Richard was constantly in motion, seeming single-handedly to surround his antagonists, using his intensely poetic language to taunt and harass them.

In this last respect, Shaw's antagonists might have been seen to include the audience as well. With the possible exceptions of 'I give this heavy weight from off my head', discussed above, and parts of the prison speech in V.v, Shaw made virtually no concessions to the metrical structure of Shakespeare's poetry. Shaw was certainly the most aggressive violator of rules for poetic speaking, but she was by no means the only actor to speak unmetrically; in the semi-naturalistic world Warner's production attempted to create, where the audience was asked to consider artifice as an impediment to emotional expression and engagement, rigorous verse-speaking could serve little purpose. Many reviewers noted that Warner's production showed no reverence for Shakespeare's poetry, and that Shaw not only spoke unmetrically but accompanied her speech with excessive gestures, always offering the spectator distractions from the importance of the words. Such a complaint is in many ways 'old-fashioned': journalistic reviewers often make it simply as a way of establishing their credentials in Shakespearean discourse. Academic reviewers of the last 20 years or so, working in an intellectual climate that in some ways undervalues the importance of form, generally avoid talking about an actor's verse-speaking: as though it were a highly specialized skill with which we cannot expect modern actors *necessarily* to be concerned, especially since dramatic verse is a novelty rather than a norm for modern audiences. But, for the purposes of my argument, Shaw's deliberately unpleasant verse-speaking is worth dwelling on a bit: the production's aggressive attitude toward poetry was part of its aggressive, subversive attitude toward the play – and an audience's *idea* of the play – itself.

'Not all the water in the rough rude sea / Can wash the balm off from an anointed king', Richard says at III.ii.54–5. The first of these two lines can scan perfectly iambically, and requires no internal pause (capital letters represent accented syllables in the quotations below):

Not ALL the WAter IN the ROUGH rude SEA

The second line has 11 syllables, and requires a slight collapsing of 'an' and 'anointed' in order to scan iambically:

Can WASH the BALM off FROM [an]anOINTed KING.

Like line 54, line 55 contains no internal pause; the two lines constitute a single syntactic unit, with the subject in the first and the predicate in the second; they are enjambed – the move toward the verb at the beginning of line 55 impels a speaker to run over the end of line 54 without stopping. This is how I heard Fiona Shaw pronounce these lines (a single | represents a short pause and || represents a longer pause):

Not ALLLL the WAter | in the ROUGH | RUDE SEA ||
Can WASSSSH the BALLLLM off || from an anOINTed king.

My typographical exaggerations are meant to represent the way in which Shaw exaggerated the emphases of the line; the multiple pauses, working against both syntactic expectation and aural comprehension, made the exaggerations, the lengthening of important words (for example, *wash* and *balm*) and the elision of unimportant words (*off from an*) all the more noticeable. Besides the violence done to the metre, these lines were spoken at top volume. The treatment of these lines was absolutely typical of Shaw's treatment of most of the play's lyrical lines, and as such can be seen to constitute deliberate interpretive strategy – one that is, I will argue, contiguous with the interpretive strategy constituted by the play's casting of a woman in the role of Richard.

Writing in *The Times* on 5 June 1995, Benedict Nightingale said that Warner's production, and particularly Shaw's performance,

> daring and fascinating though it is, pushes a defensible reading a mile or so too far. The grace and wit that Shakespeare gave Richard, the class and lustre even his enemies attribute to him, are almost entirely missing. Moreover, the play's core question, which is whether and at what point a divinely sanctioned king can be deposed, loses its subtlety. A ruler who sits and sucks his thumb when troubles threaten should not merely lose his job but be sent back to the nursery.

In one way of thinking, I concur entirely with Nightingale's assessment of the production, and many spectators and critics did as well. At the same time, Nightingale's subjunctive first clause, 'the performance, daring and fascinating *though it is*' is worth interrogating a bit in order to get at the heart of Warner's production's intended subversiveness. Nightingale's *though it is* suggests that, for him, three electrifying and surprising hours in the theatrical present is not enough. What he, and the critical spectators for whom he implicitly and explicitly speaks, requires is evident, precise correspondence between elements of the theatrical present and different kinds of *past* experience – other performances (Richard has been more effectively portrayed by male actors), encounters with the play as readers (Richard is represented differently by Shakespeare in the text), and encounters with historical ideas that underlie the play ('divinely sanctioned king' is a term worth taking seriously).

Nightingale and those of us who think like him might be said to want to think like Richard: we want to see at least the possibility that there is, or at some point *was*, a correspondence between what a king seems to be and what a king is. In a radical interpretation that was at once cynical and idealistic, and was perhaps the only way to approximate the effect critics have imagined a play like *Richard II* might have had on audiences for whom 'divine right' was to some extent a practical reality, Warner and Shaw attempted to deny spectators and critics any access to this kind of correspondence. For Warner and Shaw, there is no 'right way' to speak Shakespeare, there is no absolute necessity that the gender of the actor match the gender of the character, and the word *king* has always been nothing more than a word. But this radical view of the play depends for its force upon a belief in the power of its opposite, and for this reason it is important that in press interviews before and during the show's run, Warner and Shaw were hugely, deliberately imprecise when asked to analyze their own work. Insisting, as they frequently did, that the decision to cross-cast the role was 'not about gender', Fiona Shaw told an interviewer for the *Guardian* (31 May 1995) 'If you look at mankind from space you've just got two legs and two arms and nothingness. One doesn't have to swap one's thought fundamentally to deal with that.' Having established, in however bizarre a manner, that the essence of *Richard II* is a kind of universality, Shaw in the next breath becomes historically and politically particular: 'I'm very moved by the play:

the folly of the king is so particular because it affects so many people. It's all about the rituals of elevation and withdrawal.' At this point Warner chimes in, moving back in the opposite direction – and, in fact, away from Richard II entirely: 'with the great Shakespearean heroes, you're not aware of the man in them. Coriolanus is indeed a man, but Prospero or Lear – they're about being human'.

As with the tonal shifts in IV.i or the defiance of metrical regularity throughout, Warner and Shaw refused to commit to a view of their production as either tearing something down or giving new support to an ancient structure. Thus on one hand the program notes contain a quotation from Hugh Whitemore's play *Breaking the Code* – a play about the British mathematician who broke the Nazi Enigma code but was driven to suicide after the revelation of his homosexuality; citing this play would seem to suggest that what is at stake in casting a woman in the role of Richard II is a critique of twentieth-century constructions of militarism and manhood. But on the same page there is a quotation from Marjorie Garber that flies in the face of the politicized particularity suggested by the Whitemore quotation: 'transvestism and theater are interrelated, not merely "historically" or "culturally," but psychoanalytically, through the unconscious and through language'. This quotation suggests that the production's innovative casting is in fact a more perfect realization of something transcendent in, or inherent to the play. Invoking universalist and essentialist views of Shakespeare's plays in order to legitimize its disdain for those views, Warner's production as a whole plays Bolingbroke to a critic's Richard, seeking out new and expedient forms of expression, changing direction and intention when it is convenient, assaulting established conventions in order to make room for itself.

Richard Pasco/Ian Richardson – Royal Shakespeare Company, 1973

For literary critics, myself very much included, the shattering of the mirror in *Richard II* IV.i is one of the play's most thrilling moments. Here, Shakespeare calls for the literalization, or embodiment, of some of the play's most profound thematic and metaphorical concerns: as Richard looks into the mirror, he sees both himself and no-one; he sees perhaps the future of Bolingbroke represented in his present sorrow, and sees the impossibility of understanding or expressing identity by means of external signs. When he shatters the mirror on the stage floor, it is a grandiloquent theatrical gesture that both succeeds and fails in its purpose: Richard's kingly shadow has been dashed in a thousand pieces, but he cannot destroy himself.

In live performance, the shattering of the mirror in *Richard II* IV.i is often anticlimactic. We do not, of course, know the size of the mirror Shakespeare would have expected his actor to use in the first production of the play, but the metaphorical significance of the scene, and the theatrical potential inherent in a large piece of glass smashing to the floor, has always made me think of this mirror as a big one. Modern productions, no doubt acting on entirely reasonable safety concerns, generally do not use big mirrors. Nor, for the same reasons, do they generally allow the mirror to fall, as it always does in my mind, freely to the stage, sending its jagged pieces flying in all directions. Rather, modern productions tend to give Richard a hand-held mirror that he continues to hold onto while he smashes it, face down, on the floor. Keeping it face down ensures that pieces of glass will not stray too far; the small size of the mirror means that the sound of it breaking is fairly muted; the actor's continued control over the mirror as he breaks it seems to mitigate the frenzied physicality the text seems to call for. Surprisingly, the shattering of the mirror in *Richard II* IV.i turns out to be a moment, where the theatre gets in its own way, and where reading provides something that performance cannot.

John Barton's 1973 Royal Shakespeare Company production made the mirror a more prominent, significant prop than it appears to be in the text, and than it generally is in performance. For example, when Richard smashed the mirror in IV.i, all of the glass fell to the floor, leaving an empty circular frame; Bolingbroke then picked up this frame and lifted it over Richard's head as he spoke the lines 'The shadow of your sorrow hath destroyed / The shadow of your face.' As Peter Thomson said in his review of the production (*Shakespeare Survey*, 27), the mirror transformed, as Bolingbroke lowered it over Richard's head and then around his neck, from 'halo to crown, and from crown to noose' (p. 153). Richard was led to Pomfret Castle with the frame around his neck, and it featured significantly in the prison scene. There, Richard was visited by a Groom who turned out to be

Bolingbroke in disguise. In an echo of the deposition scene, the two men held the empty mirror-frame between them: 'fatal twins' (this was Irving Wardle's phrase), gazing at one another across a hollow crown.

This moment in the prison scene was the culmination of an extensive and thoroughgoing pattern of doubling and mirroring that John Barton used to organize the production. Developing and to a certain extent literalizing the text's concern with *acting* – with the connection between role playing and royal power – Barton cast two actors, Richard Pasco and Ian Richardson, in the role of the King, alternating nightly; when one was not playing the King, he was playing Bolingbroke. At the beginning of the production, the two actors appeared on stage, together with an actor dressed as Shakespeare and a mannequin on which were placed the King's robes. 'Shakespeare' handed the book he was holding to one actor or another on any given night, and that actor turned to the mannequin and donned the costume of the King while the other held a mirror – *the* mirror – so that the King could watch himself dress. From the very first moments of the production, then, Richard was faced, in Bolingbroke, with a version of himself, and the inextricably intertwined fates of the two men were framed not only within the discourse of fickle political fortune, but also that of dramatic construction and theatrical role playing.

I did not see John Barton's production; it was before my time and it was not preserved on videotape. But I feel very familiar with it, because it is perhaps the most heavily textualized production of the play. That is, it has been recounted in great detail by a number of academic authors: Peter Thomson (1974), Robert Speaight (1973), James Stredder (1976), Stanley Wells (1977), Liisa Hakola (1988), and Margaret Shewring (1996). This production captured the imagination of academics at least in part because it sought, as I have attempted to demonstrate in the preceding paragraph, to dramatize and embody a literary interpretation of the play; in construing IV.i's mirror not simply as a prop but as an organizing metaphor for the play, the production appealed to a literary sensibility; it appealed to the literary critic's delight in patterns and ironies, and in the close correspondence between word and action.

At the same time, I must admit that accounts and photographs of the production make it sound and look rather ponderous, and very much a product of a bygone historical and cultural moment. Robert Speaight described how the set

> was flanked by what looked like moving stairways, although they did not move, and it was only rarely that anyone moved up or down them. ... If the staircases were meant to remind us that, in a wider sense, this is very much a play about people going up and down, the point was taken; but in fact escalators which were plainly out of order did not ... suggest the rapidity of Richard's fall and of Bolingbroke's ascent. (p. 400)

Wardle noted that the production's 'pictorial treatment' could be 'redundantly literal. Speaking of the British earth John of Gaunt can stretch out and take a handful from a conveniently placed prop; and when the Gardener promises to plant rue for the queen, true to his word he pulls a sprig of it out of his pocket' (*The Times*, 11 April 1973). Barton heavily adapted the script, cutting about 500 lines as well as adding in lines from *2 Henry IV*. The Welsh Captain at the end of act two was turned into an eight-man chorus, speaking in unison. Once the rebellion against Richard began, Northumberland and the other antagonistic nobles appeared on stage atop high stilts, 'perfectly illustrating the metaphor that the country's flowers are being choked by envious weeds' (John Elsom, *The Listener*, 19 April 1973, quoted in Shewring, p. 130). A familiar production photograph shows Richard Pasco as the King, wearing an elaborate golden robe that forms what look like wings when he raises his arms: part angel and part sun, he is frozen mid-line, his mouth open, the grainy, static quality of the photograph and a recognizably early 1970s haircut forever freezing him in a moment whose theatricality remains inaccessible to the early twenty-first-century reader.

I am, of course, being somewhat unfair, but not without purpose. Reading accounts and reviews of the Barton-Pasco-Richardson production is a fascinating and illuminating exercise in theatre history. For, as ponderous as the production's visual patterning can sound – and, indeed, as overbearing as its contemporary viewers sometimes found it – it is clear that it captivated audiences and critics in a way that is relatively rare for any production of a Shakespeare play. Significantly less stylized (if no less conceptual) productions, such as Ron Daniels's 1990 RSC production, have attracted harsher criticism. The success of Barton's production ultimately lay in that which is easiest to perceive in the theatre and most difficult to textualize: the skill of the actors.

'The risk of stylized Shakespeare is that you may flatten out characters that have been conceived in the round', wrote Robert Speaight, 'and with a weaker cast Mr Barton's dogmatic approach might have resulted in dullness. But his method of direct attack upon the audience, and the excellent speaking throughout, secured that it did not' (p. 401). Like Richard's (or Shakespeare's) own grandiloquent theatrical gesture of the mirror, Barton's visually overwhelming production was brilliantly conceived but by no means guaranteed success: the production always threatened to get in its own way. It was from the bodies and voices of what Charles Lewsen called Richardson's 'intelligent, glittering technician' and Pasco's 'artist of unassertive integrity' (*The Times*, 12 April 1973) that the production took its energy and life. These bodies and voices are, in their powerful specificity, only obliquely perceptible to theatre-goers of the future, accessible only indirectly as we imagine the life and energy they might have given to a range of clearly defined but static artifacts: a script, a golden robe, a pair of staircases, a broken mirror.

John Gielgud – Old Vic, 1929 and Queen's Theatre, 1937

The spectre of John Gielgud's Richard II has haunted productions and criticism of the play for almost 80 years. As my discussion in Chapter 4 indicated, there is a long tradition of seeing Richard as a poet king for whom the beauties of language seductively but tragically triumph over regal substance. Gielgud's rendition of the character remains the definitive theatrical embodiment of this critical interpretation: at a crucial time for both theatrical production and literary criticism, when decisive breaks were being made with the unwieldy anachronisms of the Victorian period, John Gielgud's performance focused attention narrowly on what came to be the acknowledged heart of Shakespeare's plays, the verse. Thus, although I did not see the 1929 Old Vic production – as, indeed, no living critic has – its place in the mythology of the modern English theatre means that to a certain extent it governs and defines my expectations, and my criteria for judgment, with respect to any given production of the play and, more particularly, any given performance of the role of Richard.

The Old Vic production was not initially well-received: the play was part of a season of Shakespeare at the Old Vic which was controversial for eschewing scenic or spectacular staging, and a corresponding increase in the pace of the action and the verse-speaking. Though rapidly, clearly delivered verse and fluid movement from one scene to another are today considered the cornerstones of good Shakespeare production, these principles, emerging in large part from the work of William Poel and Harley Granville-Barker, had to struggle for legitimacy against the viewing habits of generations of theatre-goers who were accustomed to a dramaturgy that emphasized sight over sound. Writing in 1939, Gielgud himself was fairly understated in his assessment of the importance and influence of his production:

> It was in *Richard the Second* that I began at last that I was finding my feet in Shakespeare…. I had seen both Faber and Milton play Richard, but, although their pictorial qualities had impressed me greatly in the part of the King, I had taken in nothing of the intellectual or poetic beauties of the play. But as soon as I began to study the part myself, the subtlety of the characterization began to fascinate and excite me. The audience became a little more friendly towards us in *Richard the Second*. We thought that we had conquered some of their prejudices, and were rather dismayed to find that most of the critics were still in resolute opposition. I was astonished, in reading the notices again … to find how unfavourable they were. (*Early Stages*, pp. 98–9)

Part of what critics were responding to in this production was the almost inevitable sense of semi-amateurism that plagued the young and under-funded company that Gielgud had only recently joined at the Old Vic. The company produced four plays in the 1929 season, with three weeks' rehearsal and a budget of 20 pounds per play (see Shewring, p. 73). *The Times* reviewer (19 November 1929) found that '[m]any of the parts, and many far above the rank of the grooms and servants, are played badly and, what is worse, listlessly, the words being so minced and mumbled that even Shakespeare is not permitted to save the actors from themselves'. And Ronald Hayman, in his biography of Gielgud, notes that much of the production's scenery 'was painted by actors and apprentices, [and] the props department was run by semi-amateurs'; actors 'had continually to wear what was provided by the ramshackle wardrobe – doublets and robes that had already been seen again and again' (p. 54).

The principal bright spot in this production was, of course, Gielgud's performance, which even *The Times* reviewer found to be 'of genuine distinction, not only in its grasp of character, but in its control of language'. James Agate said that Gielgud's performance was characterized by 'a lovely handling of the language to which one would not refuse the highest admiration' (*The Times*, 18 November 1929). The effect Gielgud had on reordering the priorities of theatre goers, from a concern with spectacle to a concern with Shakespeare's poetry as a means of conveying interiority, can be seen clearly in *The Times* review of his 1937 *Richard II* revival at the Queen's Theatre. In this review, Gielgud is understood to be the pre-eminent Shakespearean actor of his time, and the 'key' to his interpretation is a speech that expresses the play's central concern with the unseen: ' 'Tis very true, my grief lies all within; / And these external manners of laments / Are merely shadows to the unseen grief / That swells with silence in the tortured soul' (*The Times*, 7 September 1937). Critical reception of the 1937 production created a narrative of progress, where, according to *The Times* reviewer, 'this performance...is not only more mature, but simpler in construction' than the earlier one. Of course the essential idea of the greatness of the 1929 production remained, and Gielgud's handling of the language was what, in retrospect, commentators would seize upon as the crucial element of that earlier performance: 'The infinite variations of his beautifully modulated voice hypnotised both audience and actors', said Eric Phillips, who played Bushy in the 1929 production, many years later (see Croall, p. 118). Playwright Christopher Fry remembered how Gielgud brought out the 'inner music' of Richard's speeches: 'It had a most extraordinary effect on me, and I can hear it to this day' (Croall, p. 118). 'Richard II gave [Gielgud] a better opportunity than any previous part to find out how much he could do with his voice', wrote Ronald Hayman in his 1971 biography. 'In some ways the [1929] performance must have been more gripping than John's Richard II of 1938, less subtle but more spontaneous' (p. 57). Gielgud's remarkable voice, and its ability to ring out amidst and disperse the clutter of generations of accrued theatrical tradition, came to be seen over the course of the twentieth century as the perfect instrument for realizing what had lain, vital but unheard, within Shakespeare's text for so long.

It is, in part, Gielgud's voice, or critical recollections of Gielgud's voice, that reviewers and critics hear in their heads when they criticize the verse speaking of a Fiona Shaw or a Mark Rylance. As he made clear in *Early Stages*, Gielgud linked poetic beauty with subtlety of characterization – the two elements of dramatic literature that have been most valued by twentieth-century literary critics. Ironically, and perhaps somewhat predictably, the fact that Gielgud's performance freed Shakespeare's verse, and its capacity to convey complex and subtle meanings, from the 'pictorial' theatrical tradition, had the long-term effect of chaining critics' and performers' sense of the play's maximum capability to the watershed productions of 1929 and 1937. Even as early as 1937, Harley Granville-Barker found that Gielgud had fallen away somewhat from the standard he had achieved in 1929; in a letter to Gielgud, responding to his performance at the Queen's Theatre, Granville-Barker wrote,

> Everything the actor does must be done *within the frame of the verse*. Whatever impression of action or thought he can get within this frame, without disturbance of cadence or flow, he may. But there must be nothing, no trick, no check, beyond an honest pause or so at the end of a sentence or speech'. (quoted in Shewring, p. 78)

More significantly for my purposes here, Granville-Barker went on to say, 'I think each character ought to have his own speech. I thought during the first half of the play they were imitating each other; then I found they were imitating you' (quoted in Croall, p. 244). The remarkable voice of Gielgud rang in the heads of the actors with whom he shared the stage, and would continue to do so quite loudly for at least a generation. Both Alec Guinness and Michael Redgrave, who performed in Gielgud's 1937 *Richard II*, would later say that they considered their own renditions of Richard II to be derivative (in Guinness's words, 'a partly plagiarised, third-rate imitation') of Gielgud (see Croall, p. 245).

In 1953, Gielgud, thinking that he would be considered too old for the role, directed *Richard II* at the Lyric Hammersmith, with Paul Scofield as the King – with somewhat frustrating results for actor and director (if not for audiences and critics, who were quite enthusiastic about Scofield's portrayal): 'Richard was John's part, he knew every comma, every line, and how he wanted it spoken, and I think he limited Paul a bit', said Peter Sallis, an actor in the 1973 production (quoted in Croall, p. 373). Scofield himself humbly expressed a similar point of view:

> the music of the verse was so embedded in [Gielgud's] whole being, that a divergence from that pattern must have been difficult for him to accept. But it was a pattern that could never be reassembled by another actor. I was probably not ready to impose my own, and perhaps never found it; but this was not John's fault'. (quoted in Croall, p. 373)

Gielgud himself became a victim of his own success later in 1953 when he reprised the role of *Richard II* at the Rhodes Centenary Exhibition in Bulawayo, Rhodesia (modern-day Zimbabwe). Performing before a foreign/colonial audience on a massive outdoor stage on which 'the simple screen scenery from Hammersmith looked toylike and ineffective' (Hayman, p. 187), Gielgud found that he was unable to do anything more than

> imitate the performance I gave when I was a young man, and the fact that I was older and wiser now didn't make me any better in the part; you can't imitate a young part with any kind of pleasure, and I realised I had done it so much better then. I should never have gone back to it'. (quoted in Morley, p. 258)

The Times reviewer in 1937 saw in Gielgud's performance a balance that no critic, to my knowledge, has found in any Richard since (or even before):

> ...the growth of the man in his despair of this world is felt to be a real growth, and the petulance of the beginning and the splendid agony of the end are linked each to each by early hints of splendour within and by late reminders of a weakness not, even in prison, wholly transcended.

Literary criticism beginning with the Romantics found this balance between petulance and splendour in the character of Richard, but Gielgud was the first, and perhaps the last, to make this interpretation seem possible on the stage. He was able simultaneously to suggest that the theatricality of kingship rested on something true and substantial, and that a dependence upon such theatricality belied a fatal weakness. He did this by means of rigorous attention to the poetic qualities of Shakespeare's language. Over and above his extraordinary craft as an actor, the peculiar cultural and historical circumstances that allowed Gielgud to succeed as he did cannot be recaptured – as Gielgud's anecdote of playing in Bulawayo vividly demonstrates. Performances such as Rylance's or Shaw's, evince, perhaps, not only a lost belief in the power of kingship, but a lost belief in the power of the performer to provide imaginative access to something outside of the audience's experience. Productions such as the John Barton's suggest, perhaps, that the only way in which a modern audience can be come to understand, value, and even come to rely upon the ritualistic power of kingship is if the theatre itself is turned into an instrument of ritual, where pattern and stylization provide the keys to interpretation. And perhaps the afterlife of Gielgud's performance demonstrates, as *Richard II* itself seems to, that, the moment of his coronation past, the king is always merely and inevitably a shadow of himself.

6   The Play on Screen

Margaret Shewring's *Shakespeare in Performance: King Richard II* provides an excellent and thorough overview of most of the major television productions of *Richard II*: the 1950 BBC production starring Alan Wheatley; the 1954 NBC live broadcast starring Maurice Evans; the 1960 BBC production starring David William (*Richard II* made up the first two parts in a 15-part miniseries called *An Age of Kings*, which condensed Shakespeare's two historical tetralogies into a continuous narrative); and the 1975 BBC production starring Derek Jacobi. Shewring does not cover the specially made video recordings of Michael Bogdanov's English Shakespeare Company *Richard II* (part of the Wars of the Roses cycle, starring Michael Pennington, staged in 1987–8 and filmed in 1989) and the Prospect Theatre Company *Richard II* (starring Ian McKellen, staged in 1969–70 and filmed in 1970), but she does discuss the stage productions at length. Because it had not been released at the time her book went to press, she also does not cover the made-for-television version of the Deborah Warner production starring Fiona Shaw. There are two, minor video productions of *Richard II*: one starring American television actor David Birney, made in 1982; and one produced and directed by an independent filmmaker named John Farrell, and performed by a group of semi-professional actors. Listings for both of these minor videos can be found on websites such as IMDB and Amazon; they are, however, very difficult to acquire and I was unable to get a hold of either one for this study.

In this chapter I discuss the Jacobi, Pennington, and Shaw video productions. I do not spend much time describing these productions, which are generally available in university libraries and other archives. Rather, I discuss some common elements between them that demonstrate how television's (or video's) naturalistic mode can be seen both to illuminate and to attempt to solve a persistent problem of characterization in *Richard II*.

* * *

Richard II I.iv is a short, straightforward, expository scene. In it we get an explicit sense, for the first time, of Aumerle's loyalty to Richard (as he narrates his farewell to Bolingbroke); we see, for the first time, Richard's interaction with Bushy, Bagot, and Green; and we hear in considerable detail, from Richard himself, about Richard's financial irresponsibility and its consequences: 'And for our coffers with too great a court / And liberal largess are grown somewhat light, / We are enforced to farm our royal realm' (I.iv.43–5). On the one hand, I suggested in Chapter 2, these lines can be rather unforgiving for an actor, precisely because they are so clear. These lines seem to construct Richard's character artificially and externally: rather than allow the historical king to speak as a plausibly self-interested person might, Shakespeare has put the judgment of history into Richard's own mouth and the result is ham-fisted satire that a modern actor or director might be happy to cut. A different view of the problem, one that attempted to take the text on its own terms, might argue that the apparent difficulty of these lines is actually the source of characterization: Richard is the kind of king who is perfectly happy to talk about his malfeasance because he is entirely unconcerned about it – a modern actor need only *play* the audacity of Shakespeare's dramatic construction. A theatre historian might focus this argument slightly differently: regardless of what modern actors and audiences expect, acting in the early modern period does not seem to have been as concerned with representing character in a psychologically convincing way as modern acting is. Richard's lines, and the relative difficulty of speaking them, are not meant to express something about his 'personality' from within so much as to give the audience essential information it needs to construct and interpret that personality from without. The actor – whom Shakespeare would have expected to be playing the part with very little rehearsal time and while he was also playing a large number of other roles – is not meant to 'use' the lines, merely to speak them.

I think that the surprisingly complex questions this little scene presents modern theatrical professionals about the phenomenology of character-making can be seen to be manifest in the way the scene was handled in the Jacobi, Pennington, and Shaw video productions. In each of the three productions, the scene was staged in a more localized setting than perhaps any scene other than the prison scene. In the 1978 BBC production, it was set in the royal sauna. Richard sipped wine and received a massage while his friends, wrapped in towels, sat in or around a steaming bath. As Shewring notes, Jacobi's Richard in this scene (and, I would add, the set itself) very much recalled another recent role the actor played for a BBC television show: the Emperor Claudius in *I, Claudius* (1976), a wily ruler perceived as ineffectual by many of his powerful subjects. As Jacobi sipped from his goblet in this scene (the only scene where he showed himself to be fond of wine – one of Claudius's notable vices), his voice and aspect briefly took on the slightly over-exuberant quiver and nervous jollity of Claudius once he finds himself relatively securely in power. The physical details of the scene, and the television history behind it, powerfully characterized Richard by external means; the lines about farming the realm could be spoken in a relaxed, almost trivialized way, and they made sense as such, expressing the casual unconcern of a powerful, decadent ruler.

In the English Shakespeare Company production, I.iv was set around a table, after dinner, Richard and his friends sipping sherry and smoking cigarettes among flickering, waning candles. The camera work here was able to establish an intimacy unavailable to a theatrical audience. Although this video was a recording of a stage production, it did not rely, as many theatrical archive videos do, on a single, stationary camera. Rather, it was filmed with multiple, moving cameras that could establish different degrees of close and distant focus. During this scene, the camera moved lovingly, at shoulder-height, around the table, allowing the comfortable gestures of sipping and smoking to characterize Richard and his friends as they spoke in low murmurs to one another. The most noticeable costume-detail in this scene was Aumerle's golden epaulettes, a sign of military and social prestige that subtly conveyed – as the text does not directly – his already close affiliation with Richard. The atmosphere of the scene was that of the smoke-filled back room crowded with powerful men dressed in all their finery – Richard in his element, entirely comfortable talking about his blank charters and farming the realm because no one who could hear him would take exception.

The filmed version of Deborah Warner's production followed in the tradition of these two other video productions in its staging of I.iv, again presenting the monarch in a unique instance of eating and drinking. Whereas most of the scenes in this televised production were filmed in a generalized location that evoked the narrow rectangle of the original stage set (with the notable exception of some outdoor scenes), this one was set in such a way as to suggest an intimate private chamber, warmly lit by flickering candles. Upon a table was a small bowl of cherries, or perhaps grapes, and Richard ate one of these as he spoke the lines about Bolingbroke doffing his cap to an oyster wench. As the Pennington and Jacobi video performances demonstrate as well, it is much easier to speak declamatory-sounding lines in an informal way if one is chewing or sipping on something at the same time. Talking while eating suggests relaxation; it is, moreover, something that 'real' people do – people, that is, who are not concerned, as theatrical characters must be, to direct their speech outwardly. Such naturalistic detail allows the scene to establish what feels like a genuine closeness between Richard and his coterie, and does a great deal of work in explaining why Bolingbroke and his supporters feel so alienated. The intimate atmosphere established by such detail allows the scene to give evidence, as does not seem to in the text, for the dangerously close male relationships Bolingbroke seems to be referring to when he orders the execution of Bushy and Green in III.i (see especially lines 11–14).

The Warner-Shaw video production went one step further in naturalistic detail than the two that preceded it. About halfway through the scene, the camera pulls back just enough to reveal, briefly, the extraordinary fact that Richard is moving about the room with a pair of greyhounds on a leash. As faithful pets of the monarch, these dogs mirror Bushy, Bagot, Green, and Aumerle as they trail sycophantically after Richard's every word. As sleek, aloof, simultaneously fragile and powerful animals, these dogs mirror Richard himself: the perfect pet for this King, they represent externally something that the audience perceives about Richard's inward character. And as stage properties, these dogs complete a remarkably and uniquely realistic setting for the scene, suggesting, even as they help to dramatize his rarified distance from his subjects, that Richard is 'human', a real person who enjoys the company of animals.

The main difficulty of I.iv in the theatre, at least for modern directors and actors, is that Richard's lines must be spoken outwardly, to the audience, as well as to his friends, and this feels heavily, awkwardly artificial. In my experience, productions barrel through this scene at a great pace, letting the laugh demanded by the final lines (where Richard says he hopes they 'come too late' to Gaunt's sickbed) do all the work of characterization. The conventions of small-screen filming, which privilege intimacy of focus and the significance of minor details, seem to have allowed the three productions considered here to make sense of I.iv's mechanics of characterization in a way that is compatible with modern acting and theatre-going habits. The dramaturgy of these scenes is very particular to the medium in which they were presented, and it is perhaps the case, at least for late twentieth- and early twenty-first-century audiences, that television is more successful than the theatre in communicating, as efficiently as Shakespeare's text seems to want to, the close relationship between Richard and the 'caterpillars' of his commonwealth. The attention lavished upon I.iv in order to achieve this level of communication might also indicate, of course, that the dramaturgical goals of Shakespeare's play are quite different from what we have made of them – and that a detailed, realistic perspective on Richard's behind-the-scenes relationships is less important to the play than a didactic, somewhat satirical view of the king, conveyed directly by making him speak the words that are his own undoing.

Further Reading

All works cited in the preceding chapters are recorded here. I have, however, arranged this bibliography (which includes many works not cited in the preceding chapters) thematically. I hope this decision has allowed me to create a selection of readings that will help the reader move not only further into but also beyond *Richard II*.

Editions

The early Quartos, and the Folio version, of *Richard II* can be accessed electronically through Early English Books Online, a document collection to which many university and public libraries subscribe. The edition of the play used as a basis for my study is the Signet Classic edition, edited by Kenneth Muir, first published by Penguin in 1963 and most recently reprinted in 1999. The most comprehensive scholarly recent edition is Charles R. Forker's Arden edition of 2002. Other good recent editions include, David Bevington and David Scott Kastan's Bantam Classics edition (2006), and Andrew Gurr's updated *New Cambridge Shakespeare* edition (2003). The *Variorum* edition of *Richard II* (cited in the 'Critical Assessments' chapter) was edited by Matthew Black, and published in 1955 (Philadelphia: J. B. Lippincott).

Richard II: Date, sources, and historical context

Barroll, J. L. 'A New History for Shakespeare and His Time', in *Shakespeare Quarterly*, 39 (1988), pp. 441–64.
Belsey, C. 'Making Histories Then and Now: Shakespeare from *Richard II* to *Henry V*', in Francis Barker, Peter Hulme, and Margaret Iverson (eds), *Uses of History: Marxism, Postmodernism and the Renaissance* (Manchester: Manchester University Press, 1991), pp. 24–46.

Bergeron, D. M. 'The Deposition Scene in *Richard II*', in *Renaissance Papers* (1974), pp. 31–7.

Chambers, E. K. 'The Date of *Richard II*', in 'Elizabethan Stage Gleanings', *Review of English Studies*, 1 (1925), pp. 75–6.

Clare, J. '*Art Made Tongue-Tied by Authority*': *Elizabethan and Jacobean Dramatic Censorship* (Manchester: Manchester University Press, 1990).

Clegg, C. S. '"By the choise and inuitation of al the realme": *Richard II* and Elizabethan press censorship', in *Shakespeare Quarterly*, 48(4) (1997), pp. 432–48.

Cooper, T. *Searching for Shakespeare* (New Haven, CT: Yale University Press, 2006).

Corbin, P. and Sedge, D. (eds) *Thomas of Woodstock or Richard the Second, Part One* (Manchester: Manchester University Press, 2002).

Daniel, S. *The First Fowre Bookes of the Ciuile Warres Between the Two Houses of Lancaster and Yorke* (London, 1595). Accessed on 22 July 2008 Early English Books Online http://eebo.chadwyck.com

Dutton, R. *Mastering the Revels: The Regulation and Censorship of English Renaissance Drama* (Iowa City: University of Iowa Press, 1991).

Fitter, C. 'Historicizing Shakespeare's *Richard II*: Current Events, Dating, and the Sabotage of Essex', in *Early Modern Literary Studies*, 11(2) (2005), pp. 1–47.

Greenblatt, S. (ed.) *The Power of Forms in the English Renaissance* (Norman, OK: Pilgrim Books, 1982).

Holinshed, R. *Chronicles of England, Scotland, and Ireland* (London, 1587). Accessed on 22 July 2008 Early English Books Online http://eebo.chadwyck.com. It can also be found in a six volume facsimile edition (London: J. Johnson, 1965).

Hopkins, L. '"Ripeness is all": The Death of Elizabeth in Drama', in *Renaissance Forum*, 4(2) (2000), pp. 1–21.

Johnson, O. 'Empty Houses: The Suppression of Tate's *Richard II*', in *Theatre Journal*, 47(4) (1995), pp. 503–16.

Longstaffe, S. *A Critical Edition of The Life and Death of Jack Straw* (Lewiston, NY: Edwin Mellen Press, 2002).

Matheson, L. M. 'English Chronicle Contexts for Shakespeare's Death of Richard II', in John A. Alford (ed.) *From Page to Performance: Essays in Early English Drama* (East Lansing: Michigan State University Press, 1995), pp. 195–219.

Orgel, S. 'Making Greatness Familiar', in Stephen Greenblatt (ed.) *The Power of Forms in the English Renaissance* (Norman, OK: Pilgrim Books, 1982), pp. 41–8.

Patterson, A. *Reading Holinshed's Chronicles* (Chicago: University of Chicago Press, 1994).

Saul, N. *Richard II* (New Haven: Yale University Press, 1999).

Richard II on Stage and Screen

Armstrong, A. '"What Is Become of Bushy? Where Is Green?": Metadramatic Reference to Doubling Actors in *Richard II*', in Paul Menzer (ed.) *Inside Shakespeare: Essays on the Blackfriars Stage* (Selinsgrove, PA: Susquehanna University Press, 2006), pp. 149–55.

Barkan, L. 'The Theatrical Consistency of *Richard II*', in *Shakespeare Quarterly*, 29(1) (1978), pp. 5–19.

Berger, H. 'Textual dramaturgy: representing the limits of theatre in *Richard II*', in *Theatre Journal*, 39 (1987), pp. 135–55.

Bolam, R. '*Richard II*: Shakespeare and the Languages of the Stage', in Hattaway (ed.) *Cambridge Companion to Shakespeare's History Plays* (Cambridge: Cambridge University Press, 2002), pp. 141–57.

Coursen, H. R. 'The Warner/Shaw *Richard II* on Television: A Review Article', in *Shakespeare Bulletin*, 19(4) (2001), pp. 37–8.

Greenwald, M. L. *Directions by Indirections: John Barton of the Royal Shakespeare Company* (Newark: University of Delaware Press, 1985).

Griffin, A. 'Shakespeare through the Camera's Eye 1953–1954', in *Shakespeare Quarterly*, 6(1) (1955), pp. 63–6.

Hakola, L. *In One Person Many People: The Image of the King in Three RSC Productions of William Shakespeare's King Richard II* (Helsinki: Suomalainen Tiedeakatemia, 1988).

Hill, R. F. 'Dramatic Techniques and Interpretation in *Richard II*', in John Russell Brown (ed.) *Early Shakespeare* (New York: St. Martin's Press, 1961), pp. 101–21.

Hodgdon, B. 'Inoculating the Old Stock: Shakespearean Chorographies', in *Renaissance Drama*, 34 (2005), pp. 3–29.

Klett, E. 'Many Bodies, Many Voices: Performing Androgyny in Fiona Shaw and Deborah Warner's *Richard II*', in *Theatre Journal*, 58(2) (2006), pp. 175–94.

Kliman, B. W. 'The Setting in Early Television: Maurice Evans' Shakespeare Productions', in Cecile Williamson Cary and Henry S. Limouze (eds) *Shakespeare and the Arts* (Washington, D.C.: University Press of America, 1982), pp. 135–53.

Martin, R. A. 'Metatheater, Gender, and Subjectivity in *Richard II* and *Henry IV, Part I*', in *Comparative Drama*, 23 (1989–90), pp. 255–64.

Page, M. *Richard II: Text and Performance* (London: Macmillan, 1987).

Pilkington, A. G. *Screening Shakespeare from Richard II to Henry V* (Newark: University of Delaware Press, 1991).

Pye, C. 'The Betrayal of the Gaze: Theatricality and Power in Shakespeare's *Richard II*', in *English Literary History*, 55(3) (1988), pp. 575–98.

Rackin, P. 'The Role of the Audience in Shakespeare's *Richard II*', in *Shakespeare Quarterly*, 36(3) (1985), pp. 262–81.

Rutter, C. C. 'Fiona Shaw's *Richard II*: The Girl as Player-King as Comic', in *Shakespeare Quarterly*, 48(3) (1997), pp. 314–24.

Schell, E. '*Richard II* and Some Forms of Theatrical Time', in *Comparative Drama*, 24 (1990), pp. 255–69.

Shewring, M. *Shakespeare in Performance: King Richard II* (Manchester: Manchester University Press, 1996).

Speaight, R. 'The Stratford-upon-Avon Season', in *Shakespeare Quarterly*, 24(4) (1973), pp. 400–4.

Spencer, J. M. 'Staging Pardon Scenes: Variations of Tragicomedy', in *Renaissance Drama*, 21 (1990), pp. 55–89.

Sprague, A. C. 'The First American Performance of *Richard II*', in *The Shakespeare Association Bulletin*, 19 (1944), pp. 110–16.

Stredder, J. 'John Barton's Production of *Richard II* at Stratford-upon-Avon, 1973', in *Deutsche Shakespeare-Gesellschaft West Jahrbuch* (Heidelberg: Quelle and Meyer, 1976), pp. 23–42.

Thomson, P. 'Shakespeare Straight and Crooked: A Review of the 1973 Season at Stratford', in *Shakespeare Survey*, 27 (1974), pp. 143–54.

Wells, S. *Royal Shakespeare* (Manchester: Manchester University Press, 1977).

Richard II: Language and Structure

Altick, R. D. 'Symphonic Imagery in *Richard II*', in *Publications of the Modern Language Association*, 62(2) (1947), pp. 339–65.

Berger, H. Jr *Imaginary Audition: Shakespeare on Stage and Page* (Berkeley: University of California Press, 1989).

Blank, P. 'Speaking Freely about *Richard II*', in *The Journal of English and Germanic Philology*, 96(3) (1997), pp. 327–48.

Booth, S. 'Syntax as Rhetoric in *Richard II*', in *Mosaic*, 10(3) (1977), pp. 87–103.

Coleridge, S. T. '*Richard II*', in Thomas Middleton Raysor (ed.) *Samuel Taylor Coleridge: Shakespearean Criticism* (London: J. M. Dent & Sons, 1960), pp. 141–55.

Doran, M. 'Imagery in *Richard II* and in *Henry IV*', in *Modern Language Review*, 37 (1942), pp. 113–22.

Felsen, K. '*Richard II*: Three-Part Harmony', in *Shakespeare Quarterly*, 23(12) (1972), pp. 107–11.

Forker, C. R. (ed.) *Richard II, 1780–1920* (London: Athlone, 1998).

Graham-White, A. 'Punctuation and Interpretation in *Richard II*', in *Journal of Dramatic Theory and Criticism*, 4(2) (1990), pp. 141–52.

Harris, K. 'Sun and Water Imagery in *Richard II*: Its Dramatic Function', in *Shakespeare Quarterly*, 21(2) (1970), pp. 157–65.

Hawkes, T. 'The Word against the Word: The Role of Language in Richard II, in Language and Style, 22 (1969), pp. 269–322.

Hazlitt, W. '*Richard II*', in A. W. Pollard (ed.) *Characters of Shakespeare's Plays* (London: Macmillan, 1920), pp. 110–16.

Levin, R. A. *Shakespeare's Secret Schemers: The Study of an Early Modern Dramatic Device* (Newark: University of Delaware Press, 2001).

Mack, M. Jr *Killing the King: Three Studies in Shakespeare's Tragic Structure* (New Haven: Yale University Press, 1973).

Mackenzie, A. M. *The Playgoer's Handbook to the English Renaissance Drama* (New York: Cooper Square, 1927).

McGuire, P. C. 'Choreography and Language in *Richard II*', in Philip C. McGuire and David A. Samuelson (eds) *Shakespeare: The Theatrical Dimension* (New York: AMS Press, 1979), pp. 61–84.

McMillin, S. 'Shakespeare's *Richard II*: Eyes of Sorrow, Eyes of Desire', in *Shakespeare Quarterly*, 35(1) (1984), pp. 40–52.

Menon, M. *Wanton Words: Rhetoric and Sexuality in English Renaissance Drama* (Toronto: University of Toronto Press, 2003a).

Menon, M. '*Richard II* and the Taint of Metonymy', in *English Literary History*, 70(3) (2003b), pp. 653–75.

Pater, W. 'Shakespeare's English Kings', in William E. Buckler (ed.) *Appreciations* (New York: New York University Press, 1986), pp. 506–19.

Potter, L. '"Perspectives ey'd awry": Artificiality as Truth in English Renaissance Drama', in André Lascombes (ed.) *Spectacle and*

Image in Renaissance Europe (Leiden and New York: Brill, 1993), pp. 264–80.

Siemon, J. R. *Word against Word: Shakespearean Utterance* (Amherst, MA: University of Massachusetts Press, 2002).

Suzman, A. 'Imagery and Symbolism in *Richard II*', in *Shakespeare Quarterly*, 7(4) (1956), pp. 355–70.

Swinburne, A. *Three Plays of Shakespeare* (London: Harper Brothers, 1909).

Tillyard, E. M. W. *Poetry Direct and Oblique* (London: Chatto & Windus, 1934).

Woudhuysen, H. R. (ed.) *Samuel Johnson on Shakespeare* (New York: Penguin, 1989).

Yeats, W. B. 'At Stratford-on-Avon', in *Ideas of Good and Evil* (London: A. H. Bullen, 1907), pp. 142–67.

Shakespeare's History Plays

Berger, H. Jr 'Harrying the Stage: Henry V in the Tetralogical Echo Chamber', in Graham Bradshaw, John M. Mucciolo, and Tom Bishop, Angus Fletcher (eds) *Where Are We Now in Shakespearean Studies?* (Aldershot: Ashgate, 2003), pp. 131–55.

Brownlow, F. W. *Two Shakespearean Sequences: Henry VI to Richard II and Pericles to Timon of Athens* (Pittsburgh: University of Pittsburgh Press, 1977).

Helgerson, R. *Forms of Nationhood: The Elizabethan Writing of England* (Chicago: University of Chicago Press, 1992).

Hodgdon, B. *The End Crowns All: Closure and Contradiction in Shakespeare's History* (Princeton: Princeton University Press, 1991).

Holderness, G. (ed.) *Shakespeare's History Plays: Richard II to Henry V* (New York: St. Martin's Press, 1992).

Manheim, M. 'The Weak King History Play of the Early 1590s', in *Renaissance Drama*, 2 (1969), pp. 71–80.

Moseley, C. W. R. D. *Shakespeare's History Plays: Richard II to Henry V: The Making of a King* (London: Penguin, 1988).

Porter, J. A. *The Drama of Speech Acts: Shakespeare's Lancastrian Tetralogy* (Berkeley: University of California Press, 1979).

Pye, C. *The Regal Phantasm: Shakespeare and the Politics of Spectacle* (London: Routledge, 1990).

Rackin, P. *Stages of History: Shakespeare's English Chronicles* (Ithaca, NY: Cornell University Press, 1990).

Ribner, I. *The English History Play in the Age of Shakespeare* (Princeton: Princeton University Press, 1957).

Shakespeare's Theatre

Bradbrook, M. C. *Themes and Conventions of Elizabethan Tragedy* (Cambridge: Cambridge University Press, 1935).

Chambers, E. K. *The Elizabethan Stage*, 4 vols (Oxford: Oxford University Press, 1923).

Greenblatt, S. *Renaissance Self-fashioning* (Chicago: Chicago University Press, 1984).

Gurr, A. *Playgoing in Shakespeare's London* (Cambridge: Cambridge University Press, 1987).

Gurr, A. *The Shakespearean Stage 1574–1642* (Cambridge: Cambridge University Press, 1992).

Knutson, R. *Playing Companies and Commerce in Shakespeare's Time* (Cambridge: Cambridge University Press, 2001).

Murry, J. M. *Shakespeare* (London: Jonathan Cape, 1936).

Parrott, T. M. *Shakespearean Comedy* (Oxford: Oxford University Press, 1949).

Shakespeare in Performance

Brown, J. R. *Shakespeare's Plays in Performance* (New and revised edition) (New York and London: Applause Books, 1993).

Bulman, J. C. (ed.) *Shakespeare, Theory, and Performance* (London: Routledge, 1996).

Croall, J. *Gielgud: A Theatrical Life* (London: Methhuen, 2000).

Dawson, A. B. *Watching Shakespeare: A Playgoers' Guide* (New York: St. Martin's Press, 1988).

Escolme, B. *Talking to the Audience: Shakespeare, Performance, Self* (Oxford and New York: Routledge, 2005).

Gielgud, J. *Early Stages* (New York: Macmillan, 1939).

Hayman, R. *John Gielgud* (New York: Random House, 1971).

Poel, W. *Shakespeare in the Theatre* (London: Sidgwick and Jackson, 1913).

Schoch, R. W. *Shakespeare's Victorian Stage: Performing History in the Theatre of Charles Kean* (Cambridge: Cambridge University Press, 1998).

Styan, J. L. *The Shakespeare Revolution* (Cambridge: Cambridge University Press, 1977).

Worthen, W. B. *Shakespeare and the Authority of Performance* (Cambridge: Cambridge University Press, 1997).

Index

Note: Page references given in *italics* denote excerpted material.